THE REAL
SANDWICH BOOK

Key to symbols

≅   Sandwich with a very healthy filling

≊   Sandwich with a reasonably healthy filling

⌒   Sandwich only for special treats

V   Vegetarian

❀   Prize-winning sandwich which won an award
in She magazine's sandwich competition

This book is published as the result of a
competition organised by She magazine and
the American Soybean Association. Many of
the sandwiches featured in the book were
supplied by magazine readers.

THE REAL
SANDWICH BOOK

Edited by Miriam Polunin
Food Editor of She magazine

Ebury Press
London

Published by Ebury Press
An imprint of Century Hutchinson Ltd
Brookmount House
62–65 Chandos Place
Covent Garden
London WC2N 4NW

First impression 1989

Editors: Gillian Haslam and Barbara Croxford
Designer: Peartree Design Associates
Photographer: Graham Tann
Home Economist: Dolly Meers
Stylist: Penny Crawford

Typeset in Sabon by Textype Typesetters, Cambridge
Printed and bound in Italy by New Interlitho, S.p.a., Milan

British Library Cataloguing in Publication Data
The Real Sandwich book.
   1. Sandwiches – Recipes
   I. Polunin, Miriam
   641.8'4

ISBN 0–85223–830–4

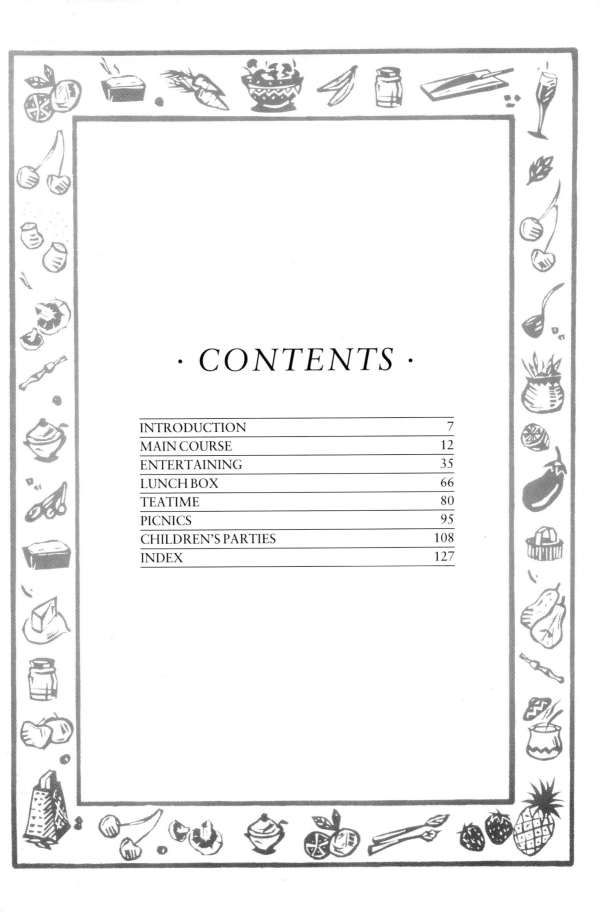

· CONTENTS ·

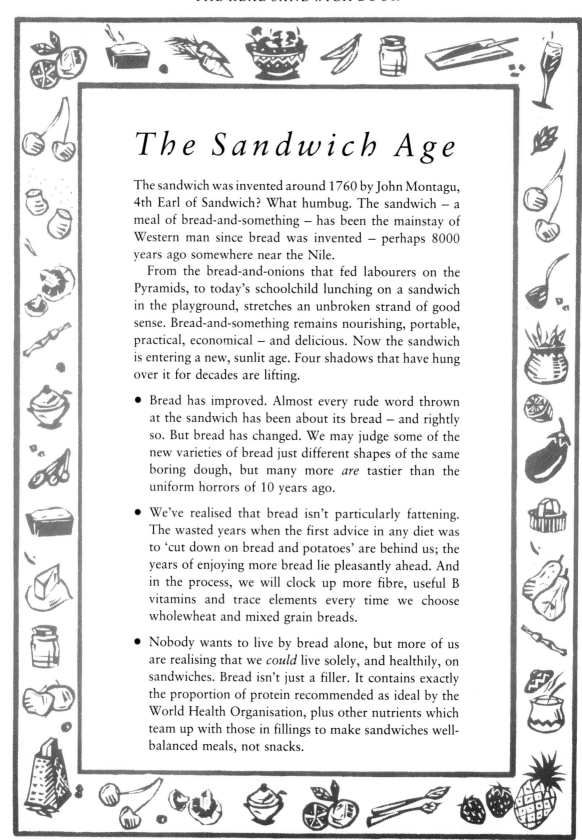

The Sandwich Age

The sandwich was invented around 1760 by John Montagu, 4th Earl of Sandwich? What humbug. The sandwich – a meal of bread-and-something – has been the mainstay of Western man since bread was invented – perhaps 8000 years ago somewhere near the Nile.

From the bread-and-onions that fed labourers on the Pyramids, to today's schoolchild lunching on a sandwich in the playground, stretches an unbroken strand of good sense. Bread-and-something remains nourishing, portable, practical, economical – and delicious. Now the sandwich is entering a new, sunlit age. Four shadows that have hung over it for decades are lifting.

- Bread has improved. Almost every rude word thrown at the sandwich has been about its bread – and rightly so. But bread has changed. We may judge some of the new varieties of bread just different shapes of the same boring dough, but many more *are* tastier than the uniform horrors of 10 years ago.

- We've realised that bread isn't particularly fattening. The wasted years when the first advice in any diet was to 'cut down on bread and potatoes' are behind us; the years of enjoying more bread lie pleasantly ahead. And in the process, we will clock up more fibre, useful B vitamins and trace elements every time we choose wholewheat and mixed grain breads.

- Nobody wants to live by bread alone, but more of us are realising that we *could* live solely, and healthily, on sandwiches. Bread isn't just a filler. It contains exactly the proportion of protein recommended as ideal by the World Health Organisation, plus other nutrients which team up with those in fillings to make sandwiches well-balanced meals, not snacks.

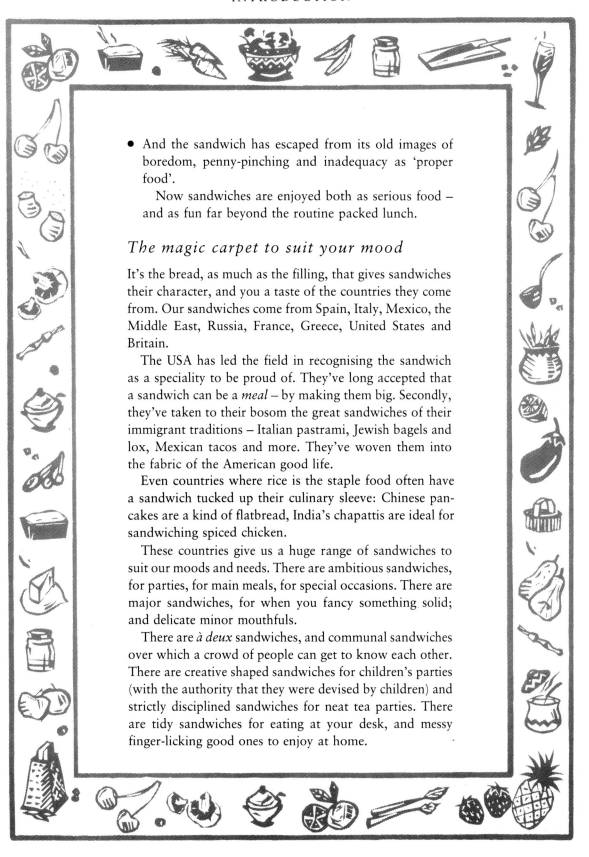

- And the sandwich has escaped from its old images of boredom, penny-pinching and inadequacy as 'proper food'.

  Now sandwiches are enjoyed both as serious food – and as fun far beyond the routine packed lunch.

The magic carpet to suit your mood

It's the bread, as much as the filling, that gives sandwiches their character, and you a taste of the countries they come from. Our sandwiches come from Spain, Italy, Mexico, the Middle East, Russia, France, Greece, United States and Britain.

The USA has led the field in recognising the sandwich as a speciality to be proud of. They've long accepted that a sandwich can be a *meal* – by making them big. Secondly, they've taken to their bosom the great sandwiches of their immigrant traditions – Italian pastrami, Jewish bagels and lox, Mexican tacos and more. They've woven them into the fabric of the American good life.

Even countries where rice is the staple food often have a sandwich tucked up their culinary sleeve: Chinese pancakes are a kind of flatbread, India's chapattis are ideal for sandwiching spiced chicken.

These countries give us a huge range of sandwiches to suit our moods and needs. There are ambitious sandwiches, for parties, for main meals, for special occasions. There are major sandwiches, for when you fancy something solid; and delicate minor mouthfuls.

There are *à deux* sandwiches, and communal sandwiches over which a crowd of people can get to know each other. There are creative shaped sandwiches for children's parties (with the authority that they were devised by children) and strictly disciplined sandwiches for neat tea parties. There are tidy sandwiches for eating at your desk, and messy finger-licking good ones to enjoy at home.

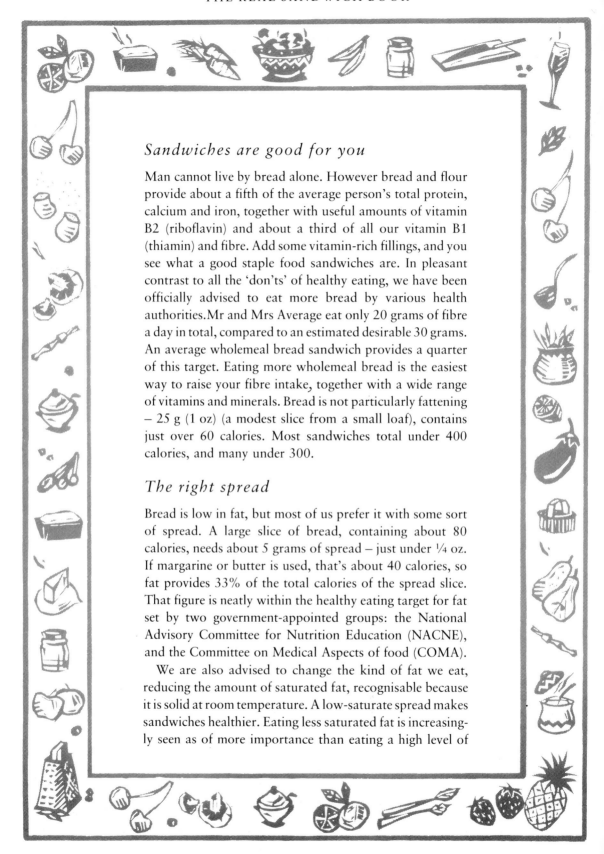

Sandwiches are good for you

Man cannot live by bread alone. However bread and flour provide about a fifth of the average person's total protein, calcium and iron, together with useful amounts of vitamin B2 (riboflavin) and about a third of all our vitamin B1 (thiamin) and fibre. Add some vitamin-rich fillings, and you see what a good staple food sandwiches are. In pleasant contrast to all the 'don'ts' of healthy eating, we have been officially advised to eat more bread by various health authorities. Mr and Mrs Average eat only 20 grams of fibre a day in total, compared to an estimated desirable 30 grams. An average wholemeal bread sandwich provides a quarter of this target. Eating more wholemeal bread is the easiest way to raise your fibre intake, together with a wide range of vitamins and minerals. Bread is not particularly fattening – 25 g (1 oz) (a modest slice from a small loaf), contains just over 60 calories. Most sandwiches total under 400 calories, and many under 300.

The right spread

Bread is low in fat, but most of us prefer it with some sort of spread. A large slice of bread, containing about 80 calories, needs about 5 grams of spread – just under ¼ oz. If margarine or butter is used, that's about 40 calories, so fat provides 33% of the total calories of the spread slice. That figure is neatly within the healthy eating target for fat set by two government-appointed groups: the National Advisory Committee for Nutrition Education (NACNE), and the Committee on Medical Aspects of food (COMA).

We are also advised to change the kind of fat we eat, reducing the amount of saturated fat, recognisable because it is solid at room temperature. A low-saturate spread makes sandwiches healthier. Eating less saturated fat is increasingly seen as of more importance than eating a high level of

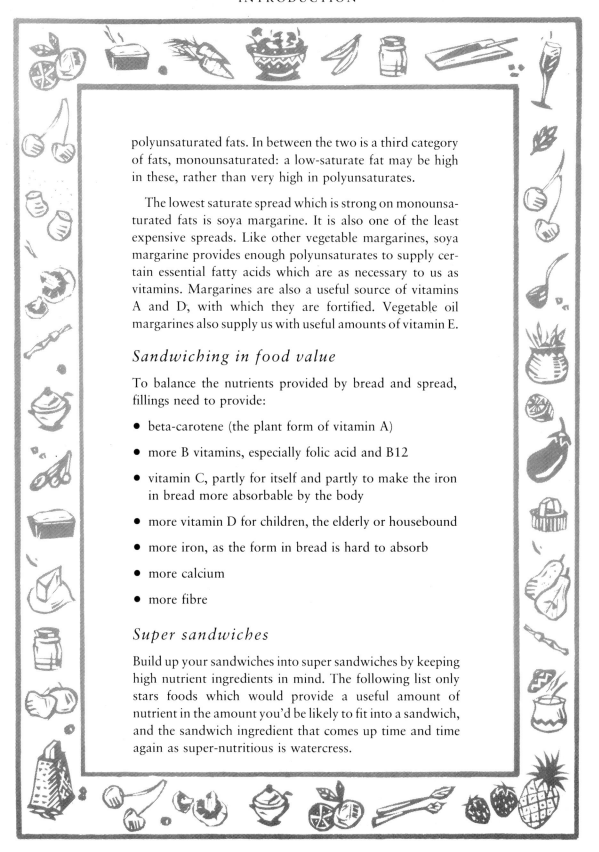

polyunsaturated fats. In between the two is a third category of fats, monounsaturated: a low-saturate fat may be high in these, rather than very high in polyunsaturates.

The lowest saturate spread which is strong on monounsaturated fats is soya margarine. It is also one of the least expensive spreads. Like other vegetable margarines, soya margarine provides enough polyunsaturates to supply certain essential fatty acids which are as necessary to us as vitamins. Margarines are also a useful source of vitamins A and D, with which they are fortified. Vegetable oil margarines also supply us with useful amounts of vitamin E.

Sandwiching in food value

To balance the nutrients provided by bread and spread, fillings need to provide:

- beta-carotene (the plant form of vitamin A)

- more B vitamins, especially folic acid and B12

- vitamin C, partly for itself and partly to make the iron in bread more absorbable by the body

- more vitamin D for children, the elderly or housebound

- more iron, as the form in bread is hard to absorb

- more calcium

- more fibre

Super sandwiches

Build up your sandwiches into super sandwiches by keeping high nutrient ingredients in mind. The following list only stars foods which would provide a useful amount of nutrient in the amount you'd be likely to fit into a sandwich, and the sandwich ingredient that comes up time and time again as super-nutritious is watercress.

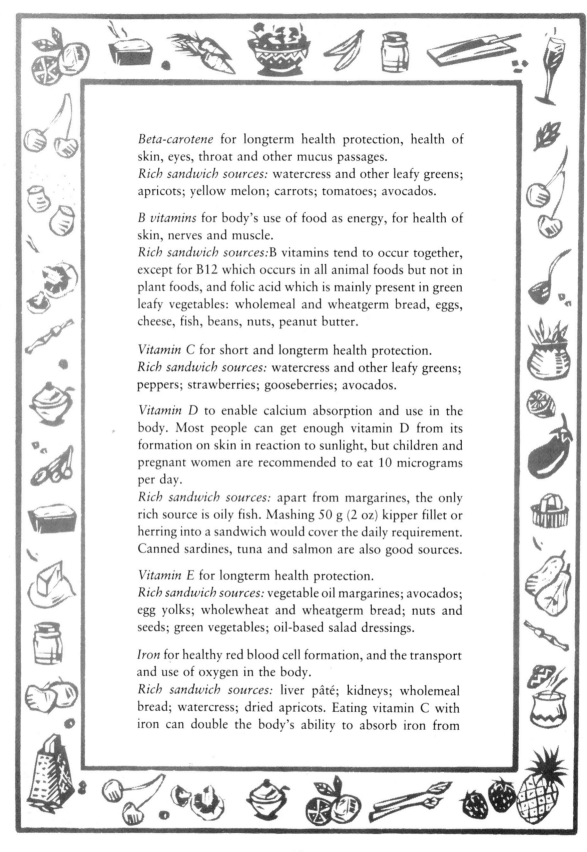

Beta-carotene for longterm health protection, health of skin, eyes, throat and other mucus passages.
Rich sandwich sources: watercress and other leafy greens; apricots; yellow melon; carrots; tomatoes; avocados.

B vitamins for body's use of food as energy, for health of skin, nerves and muscle.
Rich sandwich sources: B vitamins tend to occur together, except for B12 which occurs in all animal foods but not in plant foods, and folic acid which is mainly present in green leafy vegetables: wholemeal and wheatgerm bread, eggs, cheese, fish, beans, nuts, peanut butter.

Vitamin C for short and longterm health protection.
Rich sandwich sources: watercress and other leafy greens; peppers; strawberries; gooseberries; avocados.

Vitamin D to enable calcium absorption and use in the body. Most people can get enough vitamin D from its formation on skin in reaction to sunlight, but children and pregnant women are recommended to eat 10 micrograms per day.
Rich sandwich sources: apart from margarines, the only rich source is oily fish. Mashing 50 g (2 oz) kipper fillet or herring into a sandwich would cover the daily requirement. Canned sardines, tuna and salmon are also good sources.

Vitamin E for longterm health protection.
Rich sandwich sources: vegetable oil margarines; avocados; egg yolks; wholewheat and wheatgerm bread; nuts and seeds; green vegetables; oil-based salad dressings.

Iron for healthy red blood cell formation, and the transport and use of oxygen in the body.
Rich sandwich sources: liver pâté; kidneys; wholemeal bread; watercress; dried apricots. Eating vitamin C with iron can double the body's ability to absorb iron from

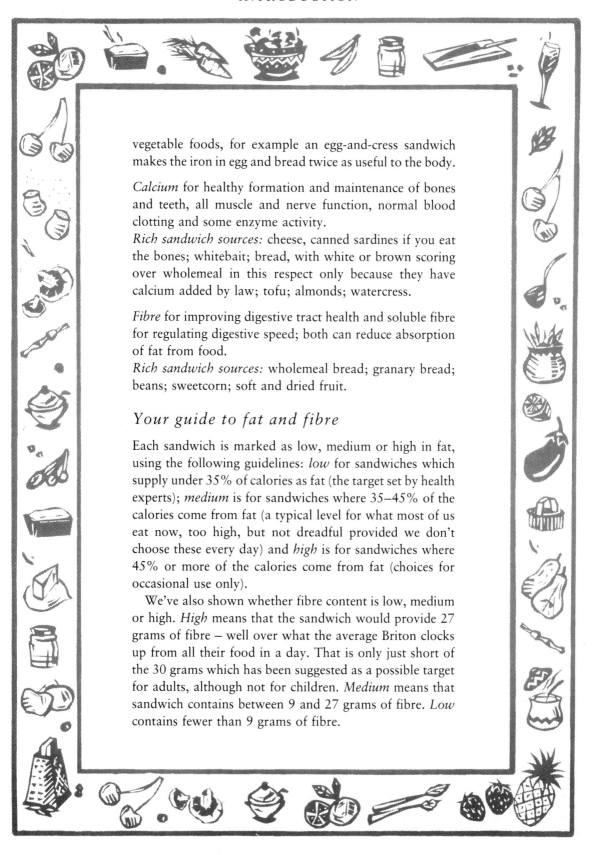

vegetable foods, for example an egg-and-cress sandwich makes the iron in egg and bread twice as useful to the body.

Calcium for healthy formation and maintenance of bones and teeth, all muscle and nerve function, normal blood clotting and some enzyme activity.
Rich sandwich sources: cheese, canned sardines if you eat the bones; whitebait; bread, with white or brown scoring over wholemeal in this respect only because they have calcium added by law; tofu; almonds; watercress.

Fibre for improving digestive tract health and soluble fibre for regulating digestive speed; both can reduce absorption of fat from food.
Rich sandwich sources: wholemeal bread; granary bread; beans; sweetcorn; soft and dried fruit.

Your guide to fat and fibre

Each sandwich is marked as low, medium or high in fat, using the following guidelines: *low* for sandwiches which supply under 35% of calories as fat (the target set by health experts); *medium* is for sandwiches where 35–45% of the calories come from fat (a typical level for what most of us eat now, too high, but not dreadful provided we don't choose these every day) and *high* is for sandwiches where 45% or more of the calories come from fat (choices for occasional use only).

We've also shown whether fibre content is low, medium or high. *High* means that the sandwich would provide 27 grams of fibre – well over what the average Briton clocks up from all their food in a day. That is only just short of the 30 grams which has been suggested as a possible target for adults, although not for children. *Medium* means that sandwich contains between 9 and 27 grams of fibre. *Low* contains fewer than 9 grams of fibre.

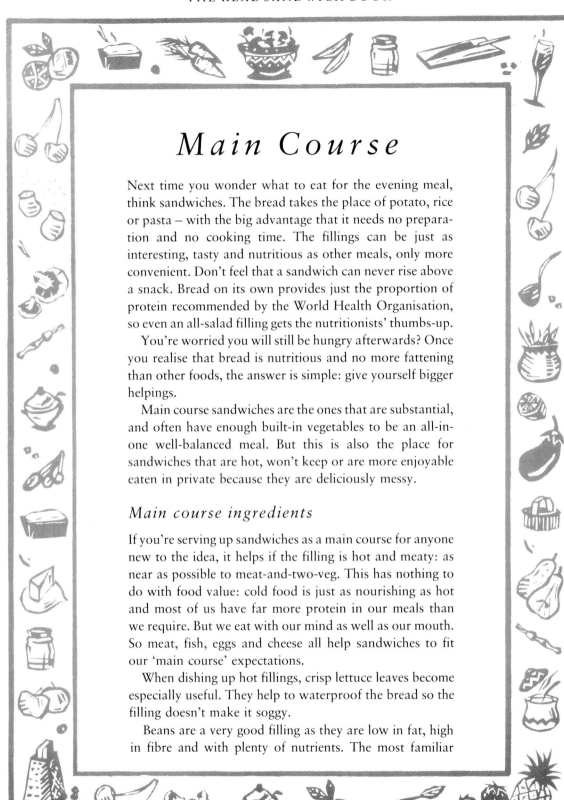

Main Course

Next time you wonder what to eat for the evening meal, think sandwiches. The bread takes the place of potato, rice or pasta – with the big advantage that it needs no preparation and no cooking time. The fillings can be just as interesting, tasty and nutritious as other meals, only more convenient. Don't feel that a sandwich can never rise above a snack. Bread on its own provides just the proportion of protein recommended by the World Health Organisation, so even an all-salad filling gets the nutritionists' thumbs-up.

You're worried you will still be hungry afterwards? Once you realise that bread is nutritious and no more fattening than other foods, the answer is simple: give yourself bigger helpings.

Main course sandwiches are the ones that are substantial, and often have enough built-in vegetables to be an all-in-one well-balanced meal. But this is also the place for sandwiches that are hot, won't keep or are more enjoyable eaten in private because they are deliciously messy.

Main course ingredients

If you're serving up sandwiches as a main course for anyone new to the idea, it helps if the filling is hot and meaty: as near as possible to meat-and-two-veg. This has nothing to do with food value: cold food is just as nourishing as hot and most of us have far more protein in our meals than we require. But we eat with our mind as well as our mouth. So meat, fish, eggs and cheese all help sandwiches to fit our 'main course' expectations.

When dishing up hot fillings, crisp lettuce leaves become especially useful. They help to waterproof the bread so the filling doesn't make it soggy.

Beans are a very good filling as they are low in fat, high in fibre and with plenty of nutrients. The most familiar

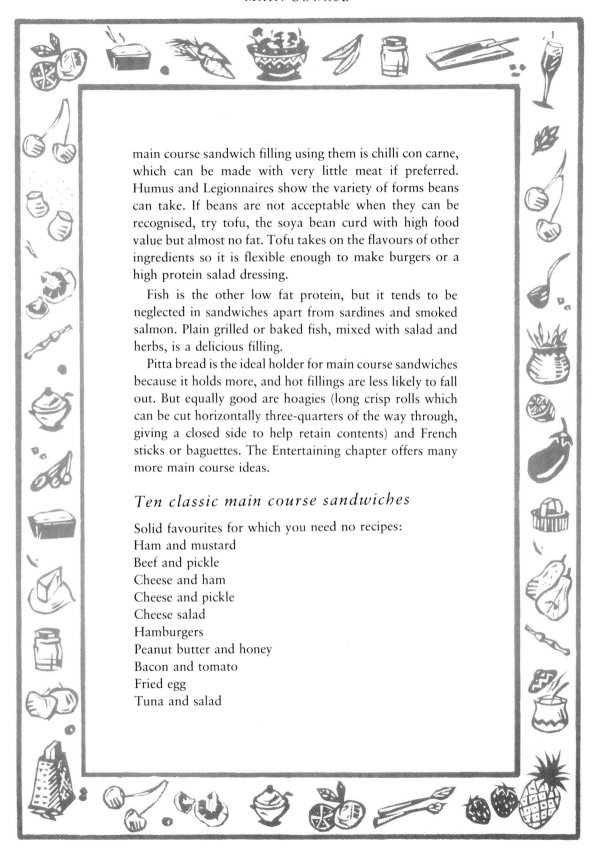

main course sandwich filling using them is chilli con carne, which can be made with very little meat if preferred. Humus and Legionnaires show the variety of forms beans can take. If beans are not acceptable when they can be recognised, try tofu, the soya bean curd with high food value but almost no fat. Tofu takes on the flavours of other ingredients so it is flexible enough to make burgers or a high protein salad dressing.

Fish is the other low fat protein, but it tends to be neglected in sandwiches apart from sardines and smoked salmon. Plain grilled or baked fish, mixed with salad and herbs, is a delicious filling.

Pitta bread is the ideal holder for main course sandwiches because it holds more, and hot fillings are less likely to fall out. But equally good are hoagies (long crisp rolls which can be cut horizontally three-quarters of the way through, giving a closed side to help retain contents) and French sticks or baguettes. The Entertaining chapter offers many more main course ideas.

Ten classic main course sandwiches

Solid favourites for which you need no recipes:
Ham and mustard
Beef and pickle
Cheese and ham
Cheese and pickle
Cheese salad
Hamburgers
Peanut butter and honey
Bacon and tomato
Fried egg
Tuna and salad

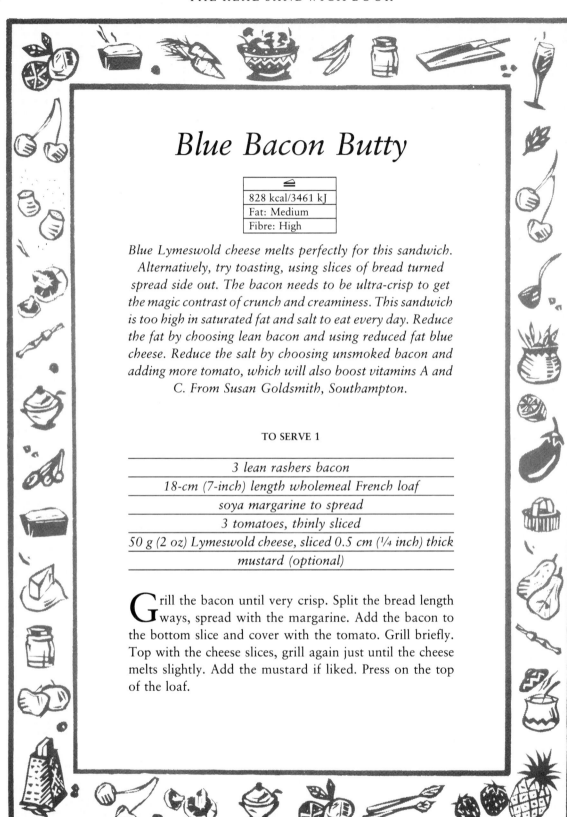

Blue Bacon Butty

828 kcal/3461 kJ
Fat: Medium
Fibre: High

Blue Lymeswold cheese melts perfectly for this sandwich. Alternatively, try toasting, using slices of bread turned spread side out. The bacon needs to be ultra-crisp to get the magic contrast of crunch and creaminess. This sandwich is too high in saturated fat and salt to eat every day. Reduce the fat by choosing lean bacon and using reduced fat blue cheese. Reduce the salt by choosing unsmoked bacon and adding more tomato, which will also boost vitamins A and C. From Susan Goldsmith, Southampton.

TO SERVE 1

3 lean rashers bacon
18-cm (7-inch) length wholemeal French loaf
soya margarine to spread
3 tomatoes, thinly sliced
50 g (2 oz) Lymeswold cheese, sliced 0.5 cm (¼ inch) thick
mustard (optional)

Grill the bacon until very crisp. Split the bread lengthways, spread with the margarine. Add the bacon to the bottom slice and cover with the tomato. Grill briefly. Top with the cheese slices, grill again just until the cheese melts slightly. Add the mustard if liked. Press on the top of the loaf.

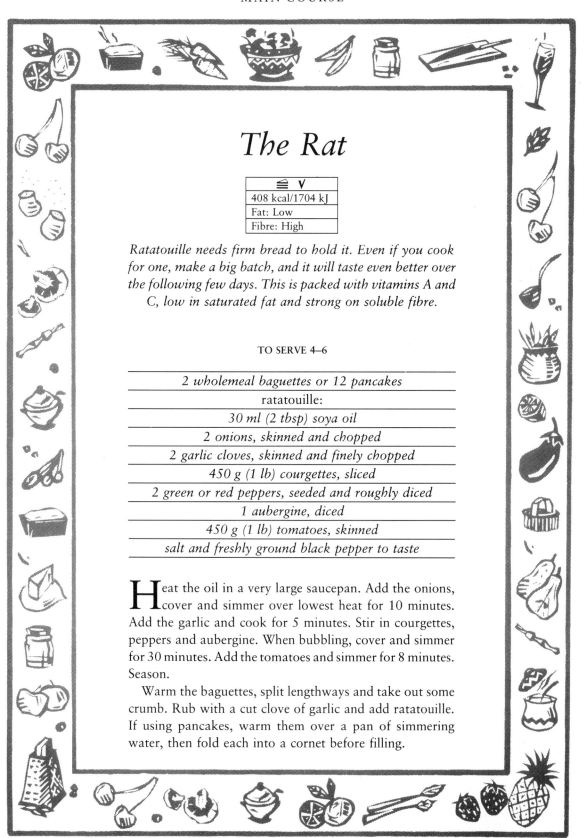

The Rat

⬢ V
408 kcal/1704 kJ
Fat: Low
Fibre: High

Ratatouille needs firm bread to hold it. Even if you cook for one, make a big batch, and it will taste even better over the following few days. This is packed with vitamins A and C, low in saturated fat and strong on soluble fibre.

TO SERVE 4–6

2 wholemeal baguettes or 12 pancakes
ratatouille:
30 ml (2 tbsp) soya oil
2 onions, skinned and chopped
2 garlic cloves, skinned and finely chopped
450 g (1 lb) courgettes, sliced
2 green or red peppers, seeded and roughly diced
1 aubergine, diced
450 g (1 lb) tomatoes, skinned
salt and freshly ground black pepper to taste

Heat the oil in a very large saucepan. Add the onions, cover and simmer over lowest heat for 10 minutes. Add the garlic and cook for 5 minutes. Stir in courgettes, peppers and aubergine. When bubbling, cover and simmer for 30 minutes. Add the tomatoes and simmer for 8 minutes. Season.

Warm the baguettes, split lengthways and take out some crumb. Rub with a cut clove of garlic and add ratatouille. If using pancakes, warm them over a pan of simmering water, then fold each into a cornet before filling.

Rat's Encore

≜ v
429 kcal/1792 kJ
Fat: Medium
Fibre: High

Ratatouille tastes even better 24 hours after it has been made. Warm the pitta bread before opening so it doesn't tear, or the filling will leak. The lettuce lining stops the bread getting soggy. Ratatouille makes a low calorie, high vitamin sandwich, especially if you use wholemeal bread which provides protein as well as vitamins and fibre. From Patricia Lambkin, Timperley.

TO SERVE 2

2 wholemeal pitta bread
soya margarine to spread
crisp lettuce leaves
225 g (8 oz) cold ratatouille (see page 15)
lemon wedges to serve

Warm the pitta bread, cut diagonally and split open. Spread the insides with the margarine. Line the pitta pockets with several lettuce leaves and spoon in the ratatouille. Serve with lemon.

Speedy Gonzales

510 kcal/2130 kJ
Fat: Low
Fibre: High

Nobody's pretending this is Mexican – but it works: a hot meal masquerading as a sandwich so you can eat it with your fingers. The lettuce leaves prevent the bread becoming soggy, so use plenty. Aim for the best quality, leanest corned beef. It's always very salty so don't add any extra. From David Lloyd, Houghton-le-Spring.

TO SERVE 3

350 g (12 oz) corned beef
large squeeze tomato purée
1 small onion, skinned and finely chopped
10 ml (2 tsp) soya oil
chilli powder to taste
60 ml (4 tbsp) canned sweetcorn-with-pepper, drained
3 wholemeal pitta bread or tortillas
crisp lettuce leaves

Mix the corned beef, tomato purée, onion, oil and chilli powder in a food processor. Place in a saucepan and heat, stirring. Simmer for at least 5 minutes. Add the sweetcorn and heat for further 2 minutes. Split the pitta bread and line the pitta pockets with lettuce leaves. Spoon in the chilli beef and serve immediately.

Wisconsin Club

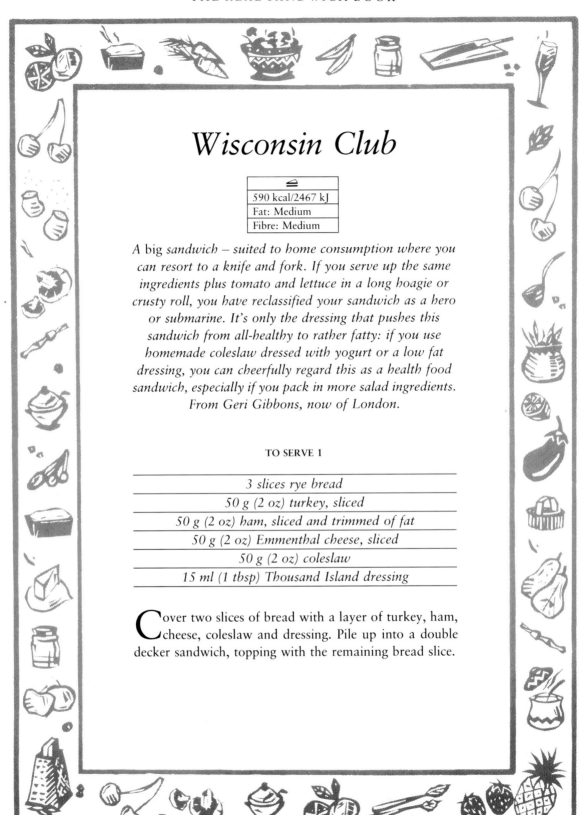

590 kcal/2467 kJ
Fat: Medium
Fibre: Medium

A big sandwich – suited to home consumption where you can resort to a knife and fork. If you serve up the same ingredients plus tomato and lettuce in a long hoagie or crusty roll, you have reclassified your sandwich as a hero or submarine. It's only the dressing that pushes this sandwich from all-healthy to rather fatty: if you use homemade coleslaw dressed with yogurt or a low fat dressing, you can cheerfully regard this as a health food sandwich, especially if you pack in more salad ingredients. From Geri Gibbons, now of London.

TO SERVE 1

3 slices rye bread
50 g (2 oz) turkey, sliced
50 g (2 oz) ham, sliced and trimmed of fat
50 g (2 oz) Emmenthal cheese, sliced
50 g (2 oz) coleslaw
15 ml (1 tbsp) Thousand Island dressing

Cover two slices of bread with a layer of turkey, ham, cheese, coleslaw and dressing. Pile up into a double decker sandwich, topping with the remaining bread slice.

Common Market

581 kcal/2429 kJ
Fat: Medium
Fibre: High

Or should it be called 'The 1992'? Taramasalata from Greece, onions and peppers from Spain, sausage from Germany, Edam from the Netherlands. You could work in something from the rest of the EEC as well: Italian basil, UK tomatoes, French walnuts, and serve on a Belgian waffle. Keep the fat level down by making your own taramasalata. Mash smoked cod's roe with lemon juice, a spoonful of the best olive oil, and low fat soft cheese. From Deborah Ramsden, Nottingham.

TO SERVE 2

50 g (2 oz) taramasalata
15 g (½ oz) soya margarine
2 wholemeal pitta bread
¼ iceberg lettuce, shredded
2 tomatoes, sliced
75-g (3-oz) piece cucumber, sliced
¼ Spanish onion, skinned and thinly sliced
¼ red pepper, seeded and thinly sliced
50 g (2 oz) Cabanos or garlic sausage, diced
50 g (2 oz) Edam cheese, diced

Mix the taramasalata and margarine with a fork. Warm the pitta bread, cut diagonally, split and spread the insides with the flavoured margarine. Place the lettuce, tomato, cucumber, onion and pepper in the pitta pockets. Finally add the sausage and cheese.

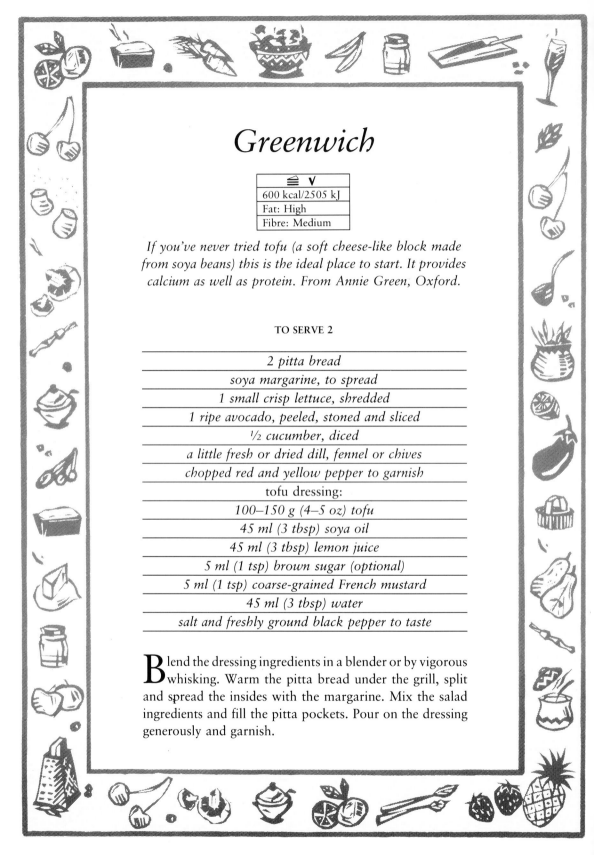

Greenwich

≦ V
600 kcal/2505 kJ
Fat: High
Fibre: Medium

If you've never tried tofu (a soft cheese-like block made from soya beans) this is the ideal place to start. It provides calcium as well as protein. From Annie Green, Oxford.

TO SERVE 2

2 pitta bread
soya margarine, to spread
1 small crisp lettuce, shredded
1 ripe avocado, peeled, stoned and sliced
½ cucumber, diced
a little fresh or dried dill, fennel or chives
chopped red and yellow pepper to garnish
tofu dressing:
100–150 g (4–5 oz) tofu
45 ml (3 tbsp) soya oil
45 ml (3 tbsp) lemon juice
5 ml (1 tsp) brown sugar (optional)
5 ml (1 tsp) coarse-grained French mustard
45 ml (3 tbsp) water
salt and freshly ground black pepper to taste

Blend the dressing ingredients in a blender or by vigorous whisking. Warm the pitta bread under the grill, split and spread the insides with the margarine. Mix the salad ingredients and fill the pitta pockets. Pour on the dressing generously and garnish.

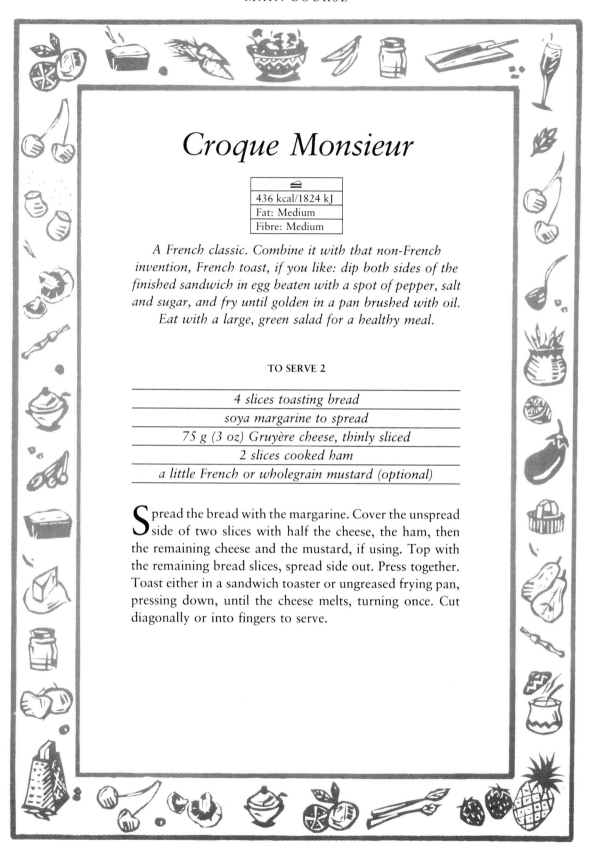

Croque Monsieur

⌂
436 kcal/1824 kJ
Fat: Medium
Fibre: Medium

A French classic. Combine it with that non-French invention, French toast, if you like: dip both sides of the finished sandwich in egg beaten with a spot of pepper, salt and sugar, and fry until golden in a pan brushed with oil. Eat with a large, green salad for a healthy meal.

TO SERVE 2

4 slices toasting bread
soya margarine to spread
75 g (3 oz) Gruyère cheese, thinly sliced
2 slices cooked ham
a little French or wholegrain mustard (optional)

Spread the bread with the margarine. Cover the unspread side of two slices with half the cheese, the ham, then the remaining cheese and the mustard, if using. Top with the remaining bread slices, spread side out. Press together. Toast either in a sandwich toaster or ungreased frying pan, pressing down, until the cheese melts, turning once. Cut diagonally or into fingers to serve.

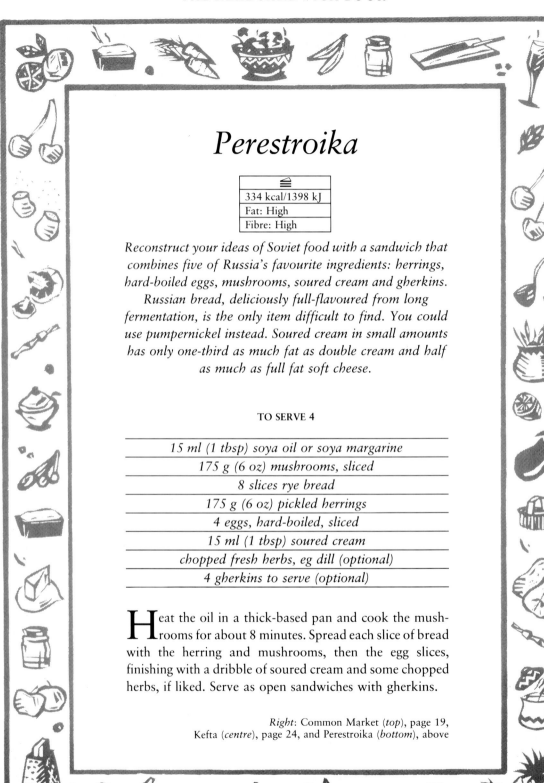

Perestroika

⬚
334 kcal/1398 kJ
Fat: High
Fibre: High

Reconstruct your ideas of Soviet food with a sandwich that combines five of Russia's favourite ingredients: herrings, hard-boiled eggs, mushrooms, soured cream and gherkins. Russian bread, deliciously full-flavoured from long fermentation, is the only item difficult to find. You could use pumpernickel instead. Soured cream in small amounts has only one-third as much fat as double cream and half as much as full fat soft cheese.

TO SERVE 4

15 ml (1 tbsp) soya oil or soya margarine
175 g (6 oz) mushrooms, sliced
8 slices rye bread
175 g (6 oz) pickled herrings
4 eggs, hard-boiled, sliced
15 ml (1 tbsp) soured cream
chopped fresh herbs, eg dill (optional)
4 gherkins to serve (optional)

Heat the oil in a thick-based pan and cook the mushrooms for about 8 minutes. Spread each slice of bread with the herring and mushrooms, then the egg slices, finishing with a dribble of soured cream and some chopped herbs, if liked. Serve as open sandwiches with gherkins.

Right: Common Market (*top*), page 19, Kefta (*centre*), page 24, and Perestroika (*bottom*), above

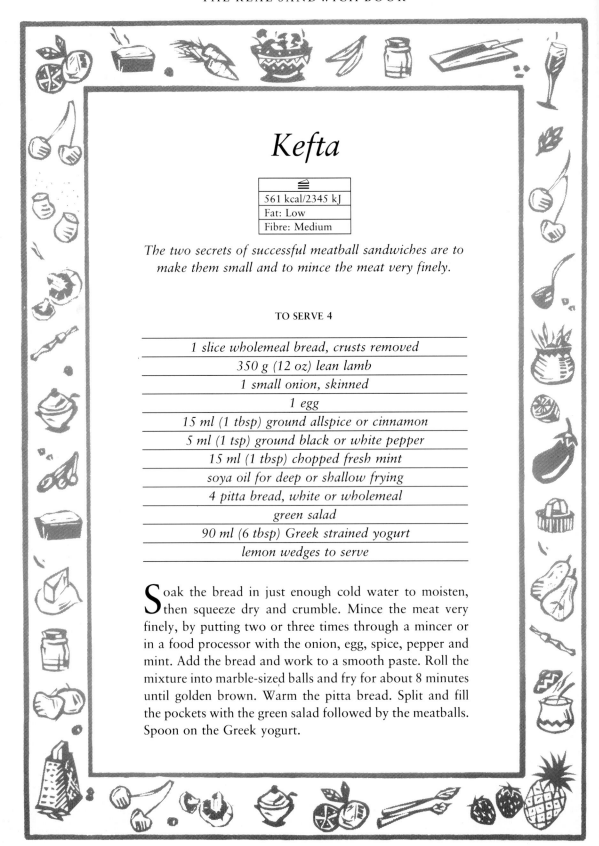

Kefta

⊟
561 kcal/2345 kJ
Fat: Low
Fibre: Medium

The two secrets of successful meatball sandwiches are to make them small and to mince the meat very finely.

TO SERVE 4

1 slice wholemeal bread, crusts removed
350 g (12 oz) lean lamb
1 small onion, skinned
1 egg
15 ml (1 tbsp) ground allspice or cinnamon
5 ml (1 tsp) ground black or white pepper
15 ml (1 tbsp) chopped fresh mint
soya oil for deep or shallow frying
4 pitta bread, white or wholemeal
green salad
90 ml (6 tbsp) Greek strained yogurt
lemon wedges to serve

Soak the bread in just enough cold water to moisten, then squeeze dry and crumble. Mince the meat very finely, by putting two or three times through a mincer or in a food processor with the onion, egg, spice, pepper and mint. Add the bread and work to a smooth paste. Roll the mixture into marble-sized balls and fry for about 8 minutes until golden brown. Warm the pitta bread. Split and fill the pockets with the green salad followed by the meatballs. Spoon on the Greek yogurt.

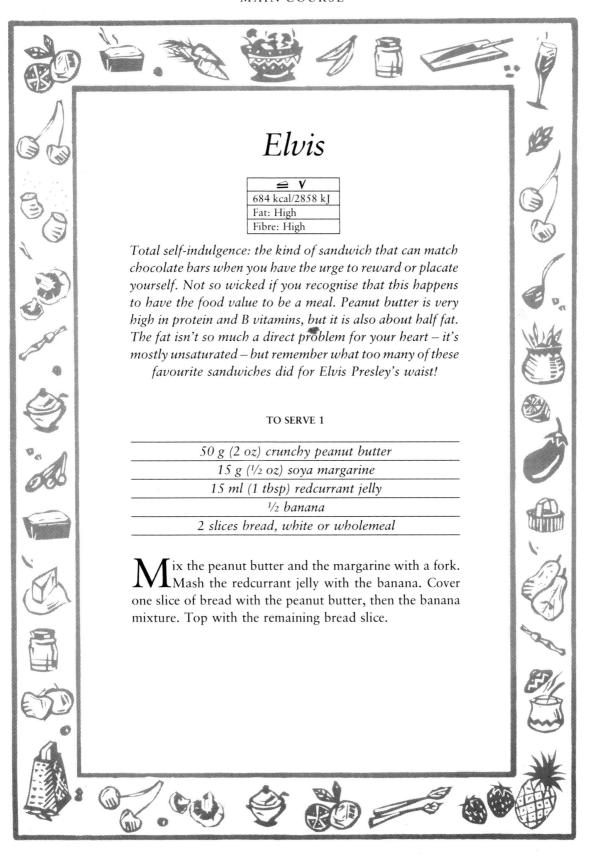

Elvis

⊵ v
684 kcal/2858 kJ
Fat: High
Fibre: High

Total self-indulgence: the kind of sandwich that can match chocolate bars when you have the urge to reward or placate yourself. Not so wicked if you recognise that this happens to have the food value to be a meal. Peanut butter is very high in protein and B vitamins, but it is also about half fat. The fat isn't so much a direct problem for your heart – it's mostly unsaturated – but remember what too many of these favourite sandwiches did for Elvis Presley's waist!

TO SERVE 1

50 g (2 oz) crunchy peanut butter
15 g (½ oz) soya margarine
15 ml (1 tbsp) redcurrant jelly
½ banana
2 slices bread, white or wholemeal

Mix the peanut butter and the margarine with a fork. Mash the redcurrant jelly with the banana. Cover one slice of bread with the peanut butter, then the banana mixture. Top with the remaining bread slice.

The BLT

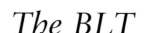

658 kcal/2749 kJ
Fat: High
Fibre: Medium

Like most American sandwiches, the BLT requires a big mouth, a big appetite and the skill to eat neatly. Easier to manage in the privacy of your own home – although they are good party and picnic food too. BLT stands for Bacon, Lettuce and Tomato. Bacon sandwiches need not be wicked if you remove most of the fat and grill until very crisp. The main problem is the mayonnaise: go easy, and choose wholemeal bread for maximum food value.

TO SERVE 2

6 rashers streaky bacon, derinded
4 large slices wholemeal toasting bread
soya margarine to spread
30 ml (2 tbsp) mayonnaise
1 beefsteak tomato, sliced
2 slices iceberg lettuce, 0.5 cm (¼ inch) thick
freshly ground black pepper to taste
8 green or black olives

Grill or fry the bacon until very crisp. Toast the bread and spread with the margarine followed by the mayonnaise. Cover two slices of bread with the tomato slices, then with the lettuce and pepper to taste. Top with the bacon and remaining bread slices, then press down. Cut into four triangles, secure with wooden cocktail sticks and serve with an olive on each stick.

Ploughman's

⊴ V
496 kcal/2073 kJ
Fat: High
Fibre: Medium

A classic lunch turned into a sandwich with the added taste of crisp apple and walnuts. The ideal sandwich in which to use the very best Cheddar – or re-discovered hard cheeses like farmhouse Caerphilly, Coverdale or one of the new goat's cheeses. Cheese is excellent for B vitamins and calcium but too high in fat to make this an everyday meal. To make a little go further in flavour, choose the best, full-flavoured cheese and grate it.

TO SERVE 4

4 large crusty rolls, wholemeal or white
soya margarine to spread
25 g (1 oz) walnuts, finely chopped
30 ml (2 tbsp) mango chutney or sweet pickle
1 crisp eating apple, red skinned
10 ml (2 tsp) lemon juice
175 g (6 oz) farmhouse cheese

Split the rolls and spread the insides with the margarine, walnuts, mango chutney or pickle. Cut the apple into thin slices, tossing with the lemon juice. Slice the cheese into four to fit the rolls, or grate coarsely. Layer the apple and cheese into the rolls and eat as soon as possible.

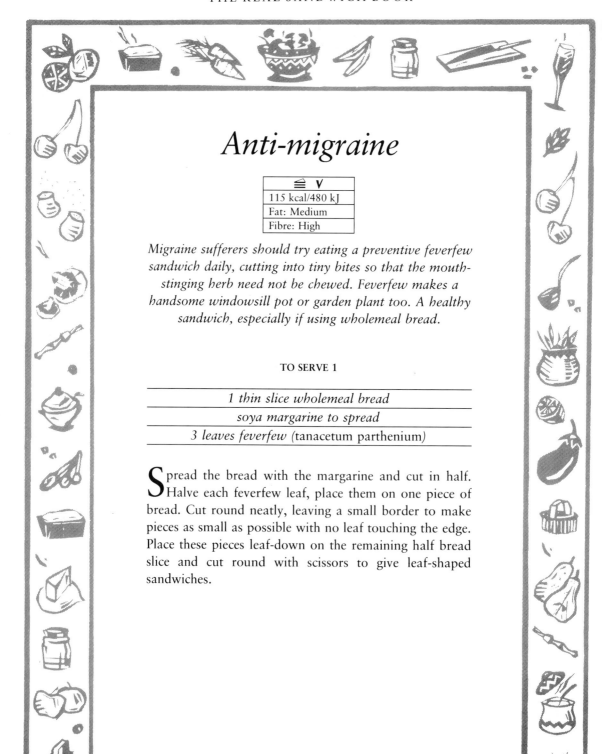

Anti-migraine

≘ V
115 kcal/480 kJ
Fat: Medium
Fibre: High

Migraine sufferers should try eating a preventive feverfew sandwich daily, cutting into tiny bites so that the mouth-stinging herb need not be chewed. Feverfew makes a handsome windowsill pot or garden plant too. A healthy sandwich, especially if using wholemeal bread.

TO SERVE 1

1 thin slice wholemeal bread

soya margarine to spread

3 leaves feverfew (tanacetum parthenium)

Spread the bread with the margarine and cut in half. Halve each feverfew leaf, place them on one piece of bread. Cut round neatly, leaving a small border to make pieces as small as possible with no leaf touching the edge. Place these pieces leaf-down on the remaining half bread slice and cut round with scissors to give leaf-shaped sandwiches.

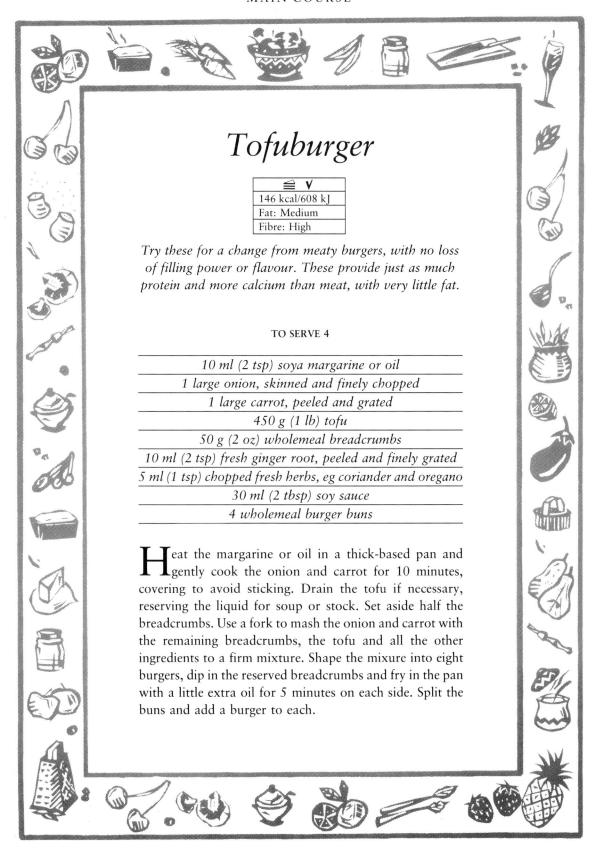

Tofuburger

⌂ V
146 kcal/608 kJ
Fat: Medium
Fibre: High

Try these for a change from meaty burgers, with no loss of filling power or flavour. These provide just as much protein and more calcium than meat, with very little fat.

TO SERVE 4

10 ml (2 tsp) soya margarine or oil
1 large onion, skinned and finely chopped
1 large carrot, peeled and grated
450 g (1 lb) tofu
50 g (2 oz) wholemeal breadcrumbs
10 ml (2 tsp) fresh ginger root, peeled and finely grated
5 ml (1 tsp) chopped fresh herbs, eg coriander and oregano
30 ml (2 tbsp) soy sauce
4 wholemeal burger buns

Heat the margarine or oil in a thick-based pan and gently cook the onion and carrot for 10 minutes, covering to avoid sticking. Drain the tofu if necessary, reserving the liquid for soup or stock. Set aside half the breadcrumbs. Use a fork to mash the onion and carrot with the remaining breadcrumbs, the tofu and all the other ingredients to a firm mixture. Shape the mixure into eight burgers, dip in the reserved breadcrumbs and fry in the pan with a little extra oil for 5 minutes on each side. Split the buns and add a burger to each.

Butterscotch and Walnut

◁ V
695 kcal/2905 kJ
Fat: Medium
Fibre: Medium

The kind of sandwich Pooh Bear would have found irresistible. Belongs in the main course chapter because by the time you have eaten this, you should not need more than a piece of fruit for pudding. There is far too much sugar in this sandwich for everyday eating – and a high amount of calories too. But an occasional splurge will do you no harm at all, and the walnuts will give you some useful essential fatty acids.

TO SERVE 4

50 g (2 oz) walnut pieces
2 bananas or eating apples, sliced
8 slices mixed grain bread
soya margarine to spread
mint sprigs or eating apple slices tossed in lemon juice to garnish
butterscotch sauce:
75 g (3 oz) brown sugar
15 g (½ oz) soya margarine
15 g (½ oz) butter
7.5 ml (½ tbsp) golden syrup
30 ml (2 tbsp) milk

→

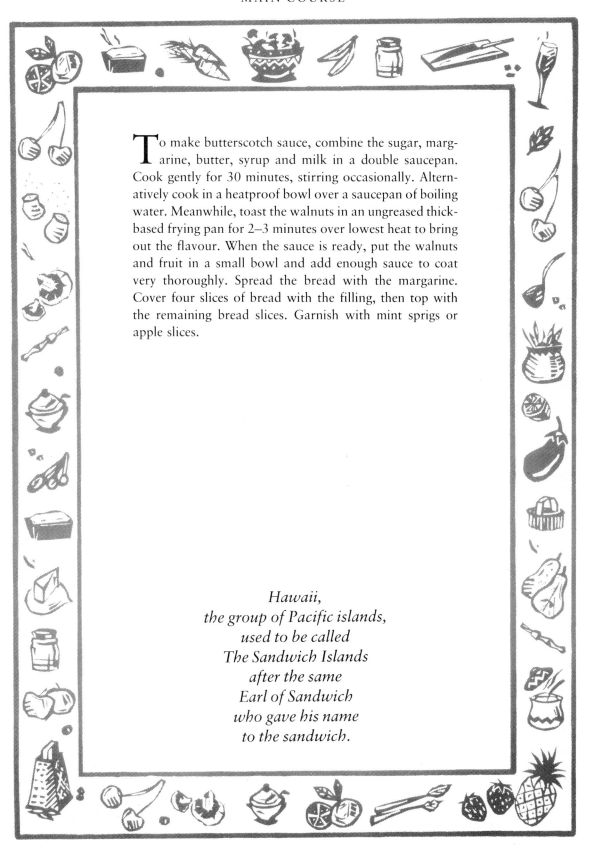

To make butterscotch sauce, combine the sugar, margarine, butter, syrup and milk in a double saucepan. Cook gently for 30 minutes, stirring occasionally. Alternatively cook in a heatproof bowl over a saucepan of boiling water. Meanwhile, toast the walnuts in an ungreased thick-based frying pan for 2–3 minutes over lowest heat to bring out the flavour. When the sauce is ready, put the walnuts and fruit in a small bowl and add enough sauce to coat very thoroughly. Spread the bread with the margarine. Cover four slices of bread with the filling, then top with the remaining bread slices. Garnish with mint sprigs or apple slices.

Hawaii,
the group of Pacific islands,
used to be called
The Sandwich Islands
after the same
Earl of Sandwich
who gave his name
to the sandwich.

Pickering

≜ V	
581 kcal/2430 kJ	
Fat: High	
Fibre: High	

*A down-to-earth North Country sandwich which would
have appeal to those arriving home hungry, hikers and
Beatrix Potter fans alike. The ideal bread for it is that
Northern speciality, barm cake – a flat, soft and floury roll.
The high food value of carrot and seeds makes this filling
in spite of the high saturated fat content of the cheese. Seeds
provide top quality essential fatty acids, provided they are
not rancid (indicated by their loss of sweetness and bitter
after-flavour). From Mrs F Pickering, Cumbria.*

TO SERVE 2

1 apple

1 small onion, skinned

75 g (3 oz) hard cheese

1 small carrot, peeled

25 g (1 oz) pumpkin or sunflower seeds

20 ml (1 good tbsp) soya spread or quark or mayonnaise

2 barm cakes or soft baps, sliced

Grate the apple, onion, cheese and carrot together or
combine in a food processor. Mix with the seeds and
bind with the spread. Split the rolls. Spread over the mixture
and toast under a hot grill for about 3 minutes until
bubbling.

Editor's Choice

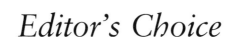

364 kcal/1522 kJ
Fat: Medium
Fibre: High

Favourite sandwich of Joyce Hopkirk, editor-in-chief of SHE magazine and a practised juggler of working life and cooking for the family. If you don't have a sandwich toaster, make two open sandwiches with the sardine on unspread side. Add top slices and 'toast' sandwich, with its layer of margarine on the outside, by pressing down firmly with an egg slice in a thick-based ungreased frying pan. The high oil content here is of a healthy kind, but still a fairly high calorie sandwich: balance the meal with a salad of vegetables, to provide low calorie bulk and vitamins A and C.

TO SERVE 2

4 slices mixed grain bread
soya margarine to spread
120 g (4½ oz) can sardines in olive oil
1 lemon

Spread the bread with the margarine sparingly. Divide the sardines between 2 unspread sides, adding enough of the olive oil from the can to moisten. Cut the lemon in half, and squeeze the juice from one half evenly over the sardines. Cut remaining lemon half into two wedges. Top the fish with the remaining bread slices, spread side out, and toast. Serve with lemon wedges.

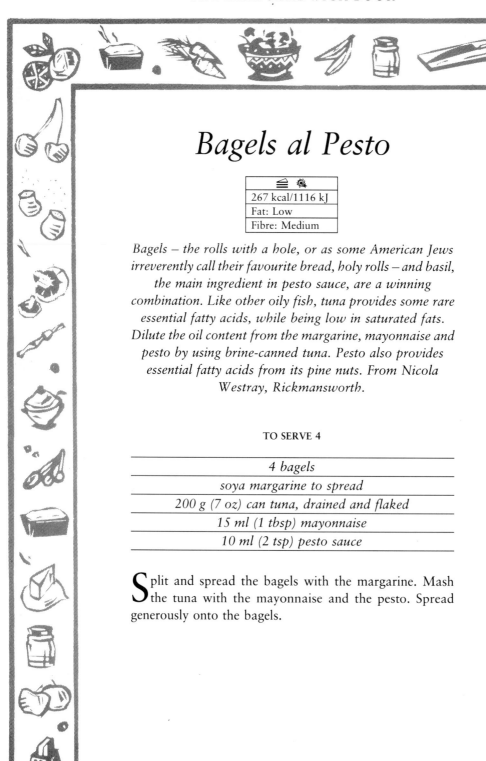

Bagels al Pesto

267 kcal/1116 kJ	
Fat: Low	
Fibre: Medium	

Bagels – the rolls with a hole, or as some American Jews irreverently call their favourite bread, holy rolls – and basil, the main ingredient in pesto sauce, are a winning combination. Like other oily fish, tuna provides some rare essential fatty acids, while being low in saturated fats. Dilute the oil content from the margarine, mayonnaise and pesto by using brine-canned tuna. Pesto also provides essential fatty acids from its pine nuts. From Nicola Westray, Rickmansworth.

TO SERVE 4

4 bagels
soya margarine to spread
200 g (7 oz) can tuna, drained and flaked
15 ml (1 tbsp) mayonnaise
10 ml (2 tsp) pesto sauce

Split and spread the bagels with the margarine. Mash the tuna with the mayonnaise and the pesto. Spread generously onto the bagels.

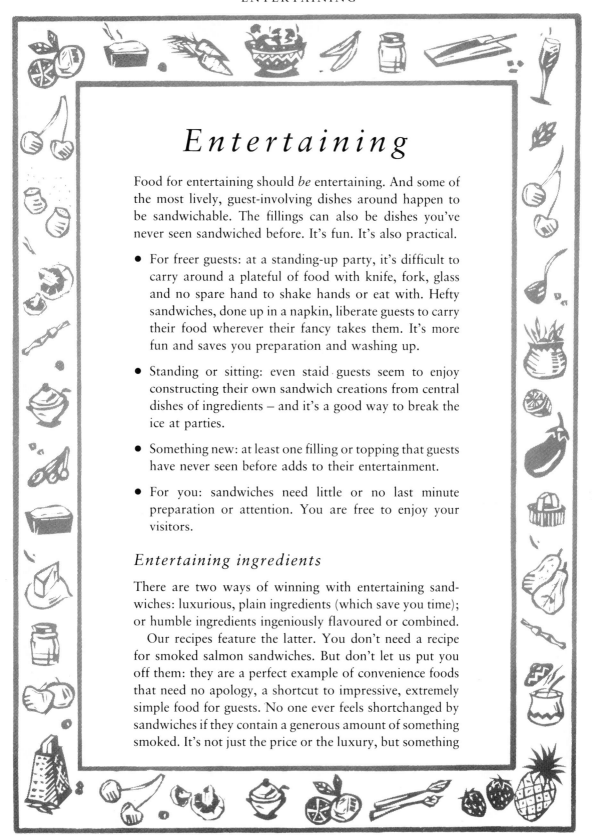

Entertaining

Food for entertaining should *be* entertaining. And some of the most lively, guest-involving dishes around happen to be sandwichable. The fillings can also be dishes you've never seen sandwiched before. It's fun. It's also practical.

- For freer guests: at a standing-up party, it's difficult to carry around a plateful of food with knife, fork, glass and no spare hand to shake hands or eat with. Hefty sandwiches, done up in a napkin, liberate guests to carry their food wherever their fancy takes them. It's more fun and saves you preparation and washing up.

- Standing or sitting: even staid guests seem to enjoy constructing their own sandwich creations from central dishes of ingredients – and it's a good way to break the ice at parties.

- Something new: at least one filling or topping that guests have never seen before adds to their entertainment.

- For you: sandwiches need little or no last minute preparation or attention. You are free to enjoy your visitors.

Entertaining ingredients

There are two ways of winning with entertaining sandwiches: luxurious, plain ingredients (which save you time); or humble ingredients ingeniously flavoured or combined.

Our recipes feature the latter. You don't need a recipe for smoked salmon sandwiches. But don't let us put you off them: they are a perfect example of convenience foods that need no apology, a shortcut to impressive, extremely simple food for guests. No one ever feels shortchanged by sandwiches if they contain a generous amount of something smoked. It's not just the price or the luxury, but something

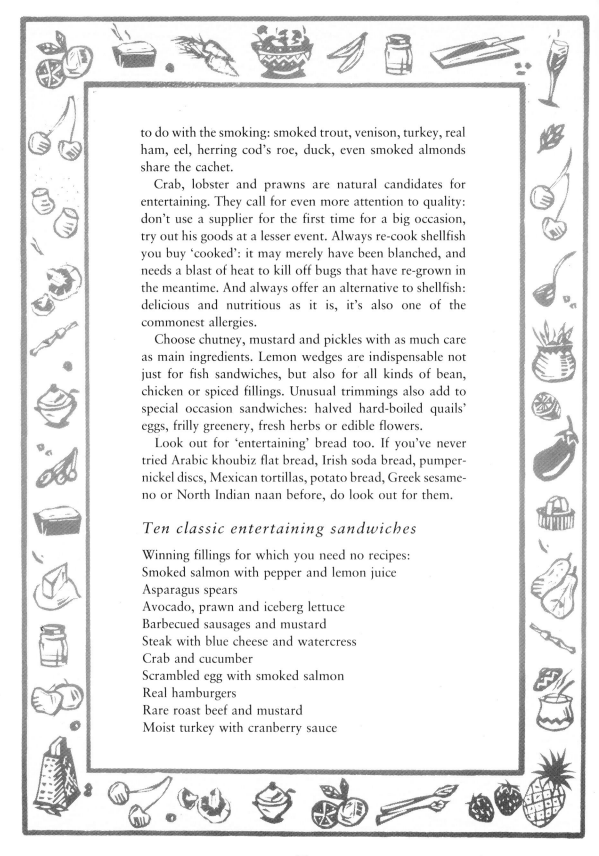

to do with the smoking: smoked trout, venison, turkey, real ham, eel, herring cod's roe, duck, even smoked almonds share the cachet.

Crab, lobster and prawns are natural candidates for entertaining. They call for even more attention to quality: don't use a supplier for the first time for a big occasion, try out his goods at a lesser event. Always re-cook shellfish you buy 'cooked': it may merely have been blanched, and needs a blast of heat to kill off bugs that have re-grown in the meantime. And always offer an alternative to shellfish: delicious and nutritious as it is, it's also one of the commonest allergies.

Choose chutney, mustard and pickles with as much care as main ingredients. Lemon wedges are indispensable not just for fish sandwiches, but also for all kinds of bean, chicken or spiced fillings. Unusual trimmings also add to special occasion sandwiches: halved hard-boiled quails' eggs, frilly greenery, fresh herbs or edible flowers.

Look out for 'entertaining' bread too. If you've never tried Arabic khoubiz flat bread, Irish soda bread, pumpernickel discs, Mexican tortillas, potato bread, Greek sesame-no or North Indian naan before, do look out for them.

Ten classic entertaining sandwiches

Winning fillings for which you need no recipes:
Smoked salmon with pepper and lemon juice
Asparagus spears
Avocado, prawn and iceberg lettuce
Barbecued sausages and mustard
Steak with blue cheese and watercress
Crab and cucumber
Scrambled egg with smoked salmon
Real hamburgers
Rare roast beef and mustard
Moist turkey with cranberry sauce

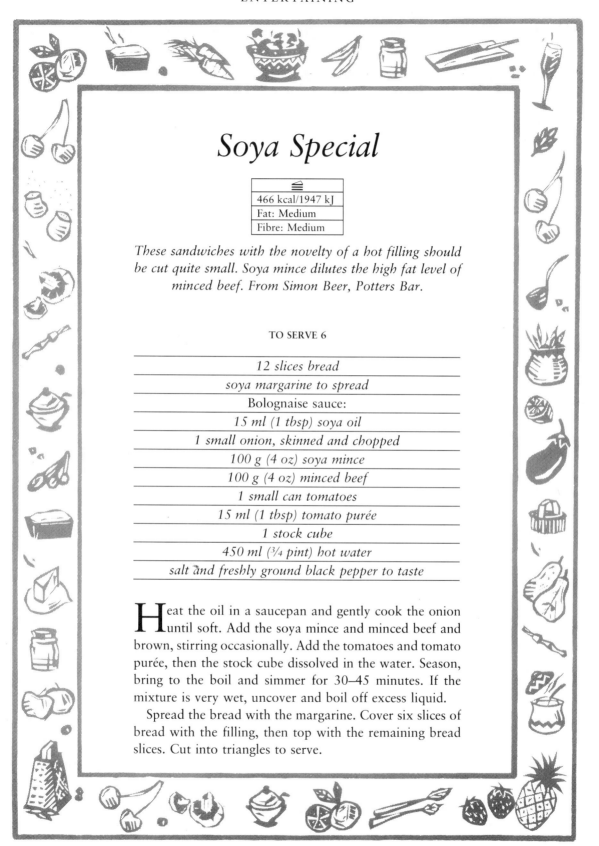

Soya Special

466 kcal/1947 kJ
Fat: Medium
Fibre: Medium

These sandwiches with the novelty of a hot filling should be cut quite small. Soya mince dilutes the high fat level of minced beef. From Simon Beer, Potters Bar.

TO SERVE 6

12 slices bread

soya margarine to spread

Bolognaise sauce:

15 ml (1 tbsp) soya oil

1 small onion, skinned and chopped

100 g (4 oz) soya mince

100 g (4 oz) minced beef

1 small can tomatoes

15 ml (1 tbsp) tomato purée

1 stock cube

450 ml (¾ pint) hot water

salt and freshly ground black pepper to taste

Heat the oil in a saucepan and gently cook the onion until soft. Add the soya mince and minced beef and brown, stirring occasionally. Add the tomatoes and tomato purée, then the stock cube dissolved in the water. Season, bring to the boil and simmer for 30–45 minutes. If the mixture is very wet, uncover and boil off excess liquid.

Spread the bread with the margarine. Cover six slices of bread with the filling, then top with the remaining bread slices. Cut into triangles to serve.

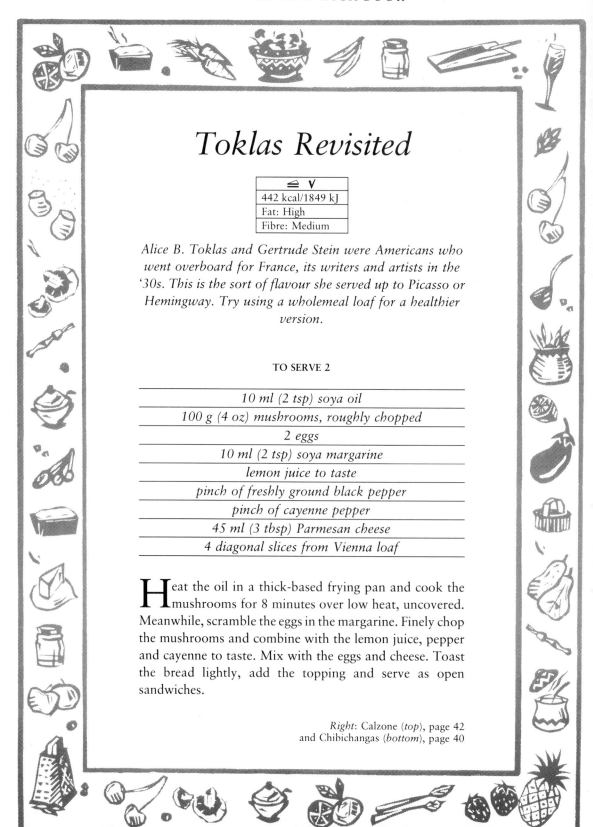

Toklas Revisited

⏟ V
442 kcal/1849 kJ
Fat: High
Fibre: Medium

Alice B. Toklas and Gertrude Stein were Americans who went overboard for France, its writers and artists in the '30s. This is the sort of flavour she served up to Picasso or Hemingway. Try using a wholemeal loaf for a healthier version.

TO SERVE 2

10 ml (2 tsp) soya oil
100 g (4 oz) mushrooms, roughly chopped
2 eggs
10 ml (2 tsp) soya margarine
lemon juice to taste
pinch of freshly ground black pepper
pinch of cayenne pepper
45 ml (3 tbsp) Parmesan cheese
4 diagonal slices from Vienna loaf

Heat the oil in a thick-based frying pan and cook the mushrooms for 8 minutes over low heat, uncovered. Meanwhile, scramble the eggs in the margarine. Finely chop the mushrooms and combine with the lemon juice, pepper and cayenne to taste. Mix with the eggs and cheese. Toast the bread lightly, add the topping and serve as open sandwiches.

Right: Calzone (*top*), page 42
and Chibichangas (*bottom*), page 40

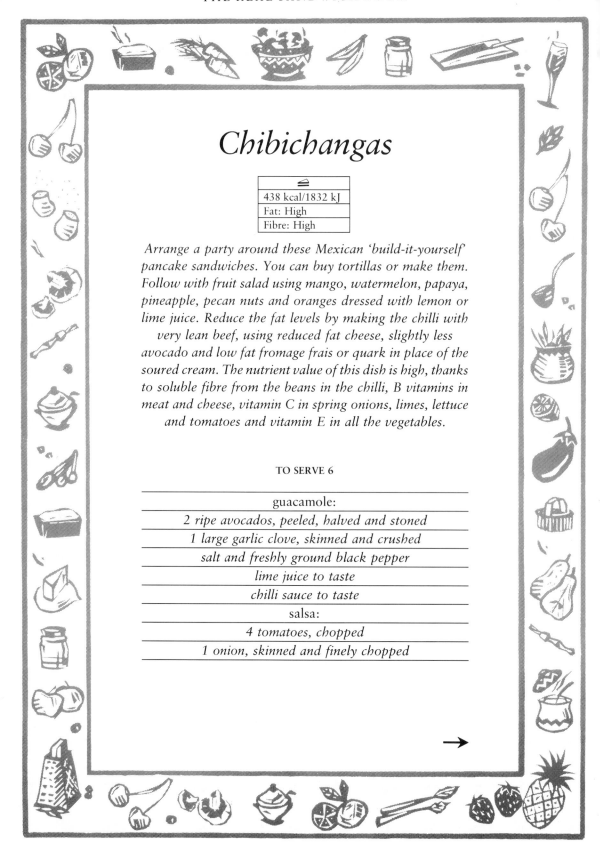

Chibichangas

⌒
438 kcal/1832 kJ
Fat: High
Fibre: High

Arrange a party around these Mexican 'build-it-yourself' pancake sandwiches. You can buy tortillas or make them. Follow with fruit salad using mango, watermelon, papaya, pineapple, pecan nuts and oranges dressed with lemon or lime juice. Reduce the fat levels by making the chilli with very lean beef, using reduced fat cheese, slightly less avocado and low fat fromage frais or quark in place of the soured cream. The nutrient value of this dish is high, thanks to soluble fibre from the beans in the chilli, B vitamins in meat and cheese, vitamin C in spring onions, limes, lettuce and tomatoes and vitamin E in all the vegetables.

TO SERVE 6

guacamole:
2 ripe avocados, peeled, halved and stoned
1 large garlic clove, skinned and crushed
salt and freshly ground black pepper
lime juice to taste
chilli sauce to taste
salsa:
4 tomatoes, chopped
1 onion, skinned and finely chopped

→

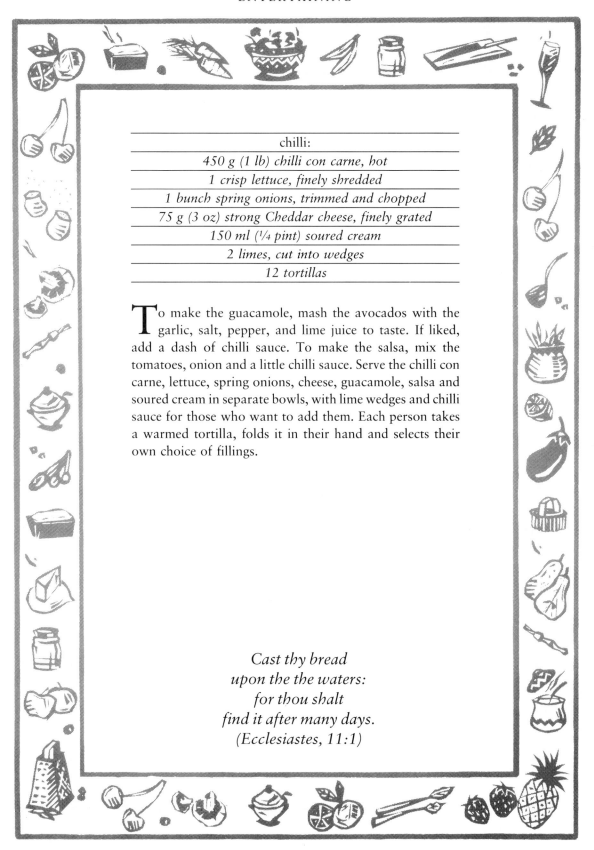

chilli:
450 g (1 lb) chilli con carne, hot
1 crisp lettuce, finely shredded
1 bunch spring onions, trimmed and chopped
75 g (3 oz) strong Cheddar cheese, finely grated
150 ml (¼ pint) soured cream
2 limes, cut into wedges
12 tortillas

To make the guacamole, mash the avocados with the garlic, salt, pepper, and lime juice to taste. If liked, add a dash of chilli sauce. To make the salsa, mix the tomatoes, onion and a little chilli sauce. Serve the chilli con carne, lettuce, spring onions, cheese, guacamole, salsa and soured cream in separate bowls, with lime wedges and chilli sauce for those who want to add them. Each person takes a warmed tortilla, folds it in their hand and selects their own choice of fillings.

Cast thy bread
upon the the waters:
for thou shalt
find it after many days.
(Ecclesiastes, 11:1)

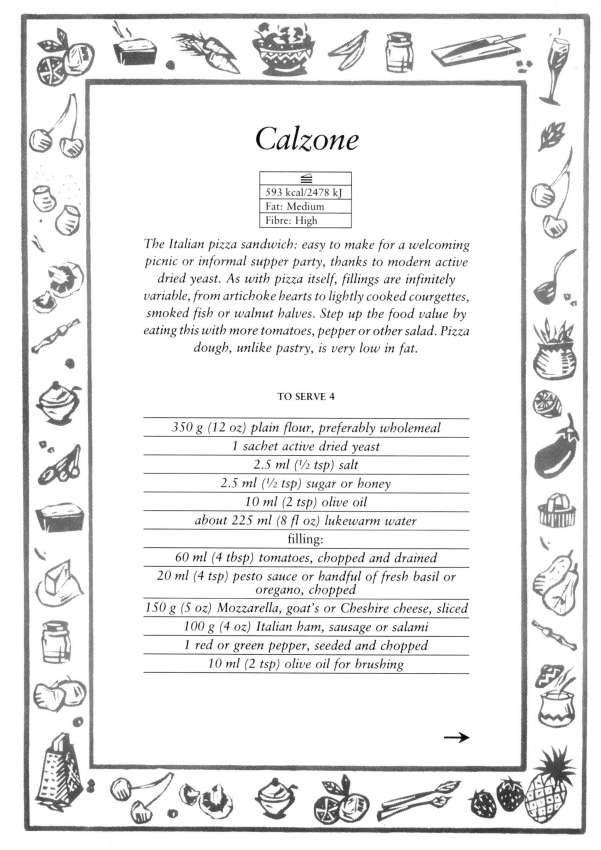

Calzone

≜
593 kcal/2478 kJ
Fat: Medium
Fibre: High

The Italian pizza sandwich: easy to make for a welcoming picnic or informal supper party, thanks to modern active dried yeast. As with pizza itself, fillings are infinitely variable, from artichoke hearts to lightly cooked courgettes, smoked fish or walnut halves. Step up the food value by eating this with more tomatoes, pepper or other salad. Pizza dough, unlike pastry, is very low in fat.

TO SERVE 4

350 g (12 oz) plain flour, preferably wholemeal
1 sachet active dried yeast
2.5 ml (½ tsp) salt
2.5 ml (½ tsp) sugar or honey
10 ml (2 tsp) olive oil
about 225 ml (8 fl oz) lukewarm water
filling:
60 ml (4 tbsp) tomatoes, chopped and drained
20 ml (4 tsp) pesto sauce or handful of fresh basil or oregano, chopped
150 g (5 oz) Mozzarella, goat's or Cheshire cheese, sliced
100 g (4 oz) Italian ham, sausage or salami
1 red or green pepper, seeded and chopped
10 ml (2 tsp) olive oil for brushing

→

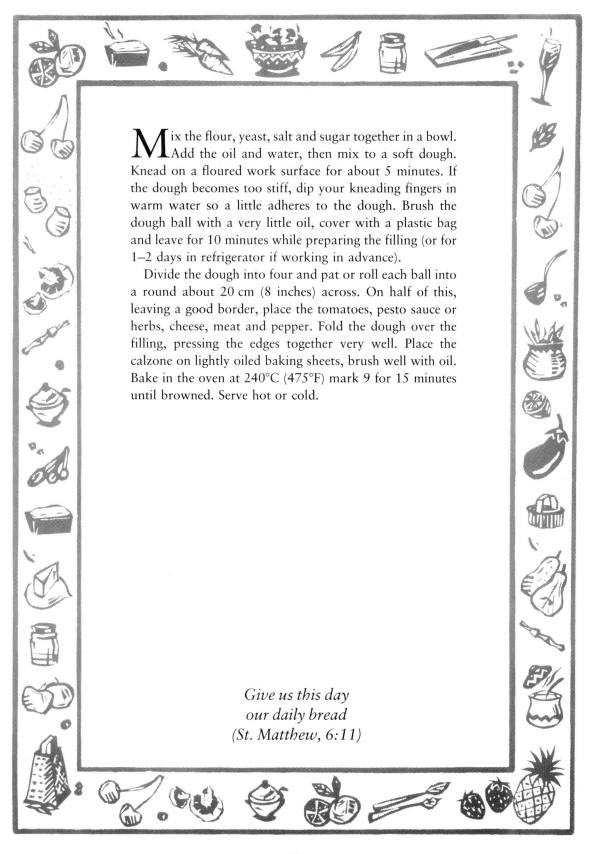

Mix the flour, yeast, salt and sugar together in a bowl. Add the oil and water, then mix to a soft dough. Knead on a floured work surface for about 5 minutes. If the dough becomes too stiff, dip your kneading fingers in warm water so a little adheres to the dough. Brush the dough ball with a very little oil, cover with a plastic bag and leave for 10 minutes while preparing the filling (or for 1–2 days in refrigerator if working in advance).

Divide the dough into four and pat or roll each ball into a round about 20 cm (8 inches) across. On half of this, leaving a good border, place the tomatoes, pesto sauce or herbs, cheese, meat and pepper. Fold the dough over the filling, pressing the edges together very well. Place the calzone on lightly oiled baking sheets, brush well with oil. Bake in the oven at 240°C (475°F) mark 9 for 15 minutes until browned. Serve hot or cold.

Give us this day
our daily bread
(St. Matthew, 6:11)

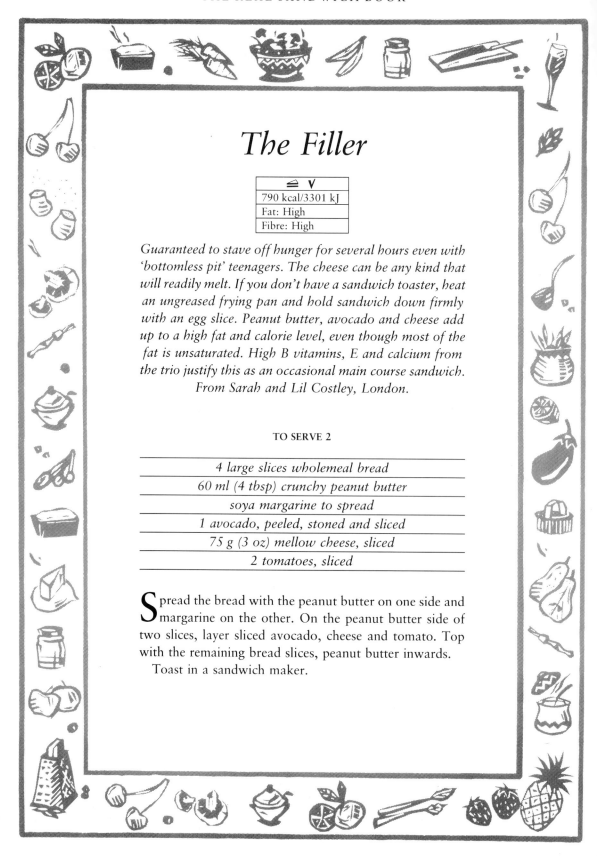

The Filler

⊜ V	
790 kcal/3301 kJ	
Fat: High	
Fibre: High	

Guaranteed to stave off hunger for several hours even with 'bottomless pit' teenagers. The cheese can be any kind that will readily melt. If you don't have a sandwich toaster, heat an ungreased frying pan and hold sandwich down firmly with an egg slice. Peanut butter, avocado and cheese add up to a high fat and calorie level, even though most of the fat is unsaturated. High B vitamins, E and calcium from the trio justify this as an occasional main course sandwich.
From Sarah and Lil Costley, London.

TO SERVE 2

4 large slices wholemeal bread
60 ml (4 tbsp) crunchy peanut butter
soya margarine to spread
1 avocado, peeled, stoned and sliced
75 g (3 oz) mellow cheese, sliced
2 tomatoes, sliced

Spread the bread with the peanut butter on one side and margarine on the other. On the peanut butter side of two slices, layer sliced avocado, cheese and tomato. Top with the remaining bread slices, peanut butter inwards.

Toast in a sandwich maker.

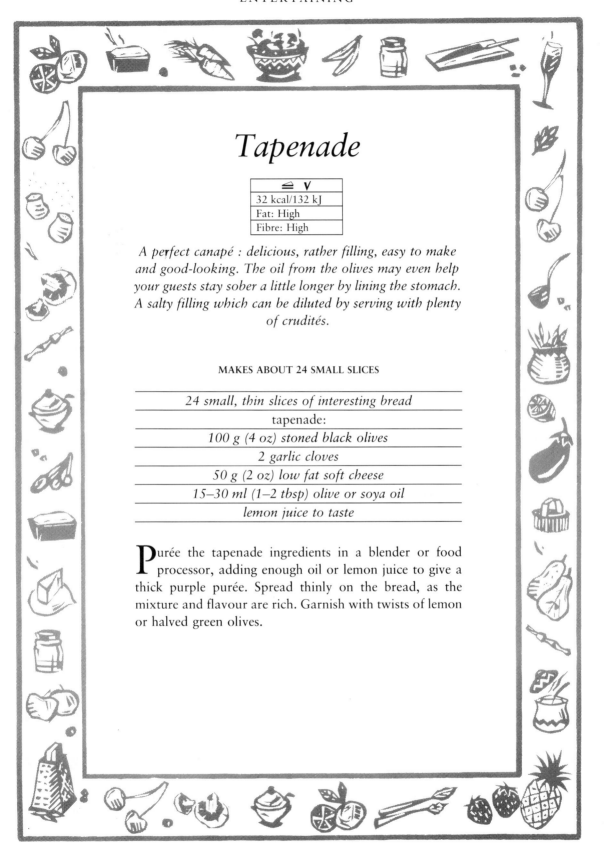

Tapenade

⊇ V
32 kcal/132 kJ
Fat: High
Fibre: High

A perfect canapé : delicious, rather filling, easy to make and good-looking. The oil from the olives may even help your guests stay sober a little longer by lining the stomach. A salty filling which can be diluted by serving with plenty of crudités.

MAKES ABOUT 24 SMALL SLICES

24 small, thin slices of interesting bread
tapenade:
100 g (4 oz) stoned black olives
2 garlic cloves
50 g (2 oz) low fat soft cheese
15–30 ml (1–2 tbsp) olive or soya oil
lemon juice to taste

Purée the tapenade ingredients in a blender or food processor, adding enough oil or lemon juice to give a thick purple purée. Spread thinly on the bread, as the mixture and flavour are rich. Garnish with twists of lemon or halved green olives.

Lord Sandwich

843 kcal/3522 kJ
Fat: Medium
Fibre: High

A good addition to a buffet, this has a pâté-like texture, and needs to be eaten with a fork. Peggy Goldrick from Stourport designed it for her racehorse-riding son who must constantly think of his weight, and called it after the man who gave the sandwich his name. Bacon is salty, but if trimmed of all visible fat, surprisingly lean.

TO SERVE 6–8

2 chicken breasts

30 ml (2 tbsp) white wine

250 g (9 oz) fromage frais with cream

225 g (8 oz) cooked frozen peas

10 ml (2 tsp) wholegrain mustard

a very little salt

freshly ground black pepper

1 large unsliced loaf, white or wholemeal

soya margarine to spread

favourite chutney to taste

225 g (8 oz) boiled smoked lean bacon, thinly sliced

225 g (8 oz) reduced-fat cheddar cheese

100 g (4 oz) pot blue cheese dressing

225 g (8 oz) low-fat soft cheese

handful of chopped chives or pinch of cayenne pepper (optional)

radish roses and cucumber slices to garnish

→

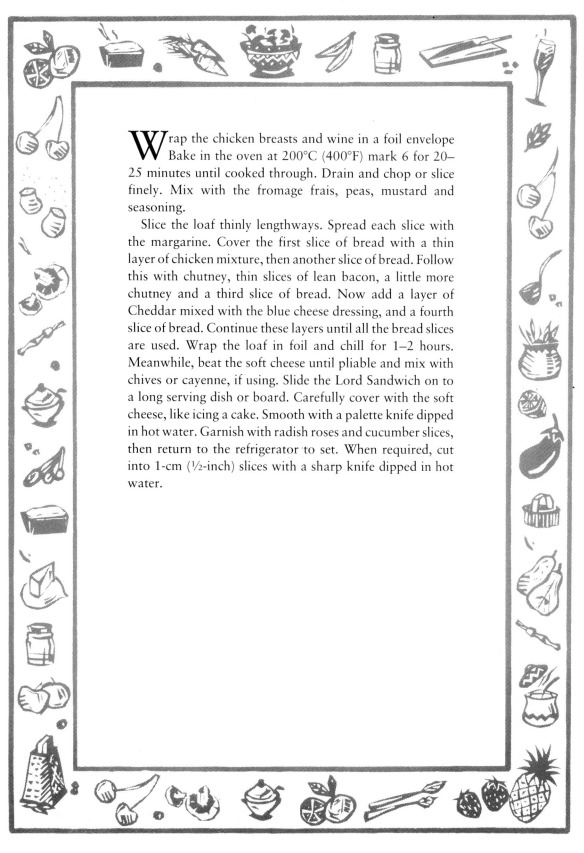

Wrap the chicken breasts and wine in a foil envelope Bake in the oven at 200°C (400°F) mark 6 for 20–25 minutes until cooked through. Drain and chop or slice finely. Mix with the fromage frais, peas, mustard and seasoning.

Slice the loaf thinly lengthways. Spread each slice with the margarine. Cover the first slice of bread with a thin layer of chicken mixture, then another slice of bread. Follow this with chutney, thin slices of lean bacon, a little more chutney and a third slice of bread. Now add a layer of Cheddar mixed with the blue cheese dressing, and a fourth slice of bread. Continue these layers until all the bread slices are used. Wrap the loaf in foil and chill for 1–2 hours. Meanwhile, beat the soft cheese until pliable and mix with chives or cayenne, if using. Slide the Lord Sandwich on to a long serving dish or board. Carefully cover with the soft cheese, like icing a cake. Smooth with a palette knife dipped in hot water. Garnish with radish roses and cucumber slices, then return to the refrigerator to set. When required, cut into 1-cm (½-inch) slices with a sharp knife dipped in hot water.

Spring Rolls

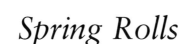

361 kcal/1509 kJ
Fat: High
Fibre: High

A stir-fried spring roll filling makes a delicious toasted sandwich filling too. Spread the margarine on the outside of the bread. Toast the filled sandwich in a sandwich toaster or ungreased thick-based frying pan. Light cooking and low fat ingredients combine to give this dish a high vitamin value with little fat, protein provided by the pancake or bread. Ideal for lunch or dinner.

TO SERVE 4

15 ml (1 tbsp) soya oil
1 garlic clove, skinned and sliced or crushed
5 ml (1 tsp) grated fresh ginger root
1 carrot, peeled and cut in matchsticks
100 g (4 oz) broccoli, cut in long shreds
100 g (4 oz) mushrooms, roughly chopped
100 g (4 oz) green cabbage, finely shredded
6 spring onions, trimmed and cut into long shreds
100 g (4 oz) beansprouts, washed
175 g (6 oz) peeled shrimps or prawns
8 pancakes or 4 pitta bread

→

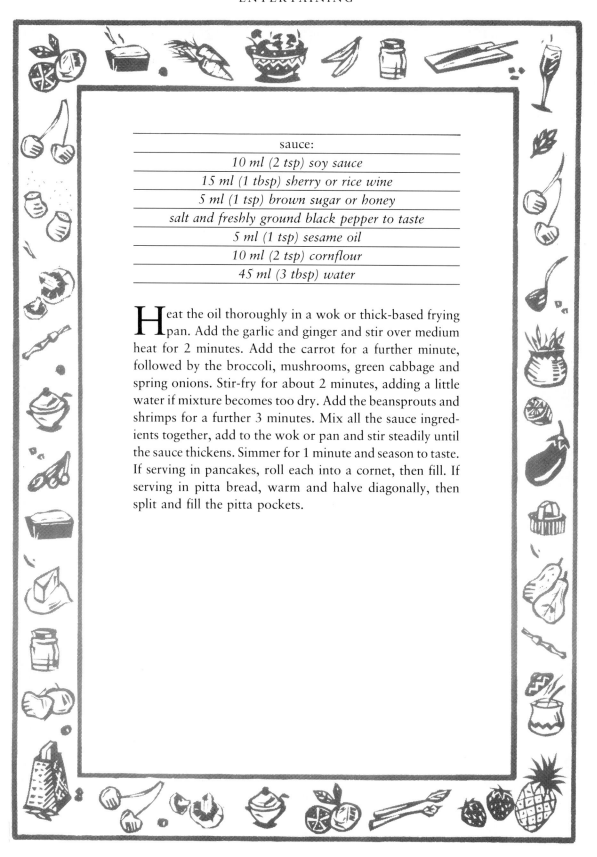

sauce:
10 ml (2 tsp) soy sauce
15 ml (1 tbsp) sherry or rice wine
5 ml (1 tsp) brown sugar or honey
salt and freshly ground black pepper to taste
5 ml (1 tsp) sesame oil
10 ml (2 tsp) cornflour
45 ml (3 tbsp) water

Heat the oil thoroughly in a wok or thick-based frying pan. Add the garlic and ginger and stir over medium heat for 2 minutes. Add the carrot for a further minute, followed by the broccoli, mushrooms, green cabbage and spring onions. Stir-fry for about 2 minutes, adding a little water if mixture becomes too dry. Add the beansprouts and shrimps for a further 3 minutes. Mix all the sauce ingredients together, add to the wok or pan and stir steadily until the sauce thickens. Simmer for 1 minute and season to taste. If serving in pancakes, roll each into a cornet, then fill. If serving in pitta bread, warm and halve diagonally, then split and fill the pitta pockets.

Olive Tapas

⌒ V
34 kcal/142 kJ
Fat: High
Fibre: High

Many Spanish tapas, from mushrooms to fish, are eaten as open sandwiches, scooped on to bread. This green olive and almond paste has a real flavour of Spain. Serve with sticks of cucumber, celery and carrot.

TO MAKE 24 CANAPÉS

1 garlic clove, skinned and crushed
10 ml (2 tsp) ground almonds
2 anchovies
5 ml (1 tsp) capers
100 g (4 oz) green olives, stoned
1.25 ml (¼ tsp) ground cumin
1.25 ml (¼ tsp) ground coriander
lemon juice to taste
15 ml (1 tbsp) olive oil
15 ml (1 tbsp) soya oil
24 small rounds of firm, interesting bread
25 g (1 oz) flaked almonds to garnish

Purée all the ingredients, except the bread and garnish, to a smooth paste in a blender or food processor. Spread the mixture thinly on the bread, leaving the sandwiches open. Toast the flaked almonds in an ungreased pan over low heat for 2–3 minutes until just browning. Garnish each tapas with almonds.

Right: Spring Rolls (*top*), page 48 and Peking Duck (*bottom*), page 52

Peking Duck

⌂
660 kcal/2757 kJ
Fat: High
Fibre: Low

Perfect for a Sunday lunch or evening party. Crispy skinned, tender duck is only half the appeal of this party dish. There's also the charm of communal sandwich-building. Detach your duck from its fat with this traditional method, and let your guests add to the oriental spirit by helping themselves with chopsticks. Even after removing a jugful of fat, duck remains one of the fattier meats.

TO SERVE 6

1 fresh duck
15 ml (1 tbsp) vinegar
30 ml (2 tbsp) honey
5 ml (1 tsp) salt
45 ml (3 tbsp) hot water
1 cucumber
1 bunch spring onions, trimmed
24 Chinese pancakes, bought or homemade, or 12 pitta bread
Chinese hoisin sauce to serve

Boil a large saucepan of water. Prick the duck all over with a skewer. Plunge in the duck for 3 minutes. Mix the vinegar, honey and salt with the hot water. Remove the duck, dry and paint with the vinegar and honey mixture. Hang up the duck in a cold dry place for at least 4 hours, or dry with a fan heater or hair drier.

→

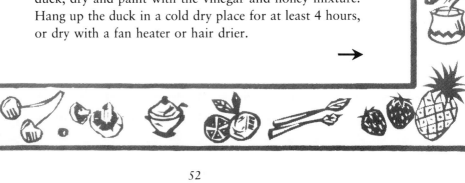

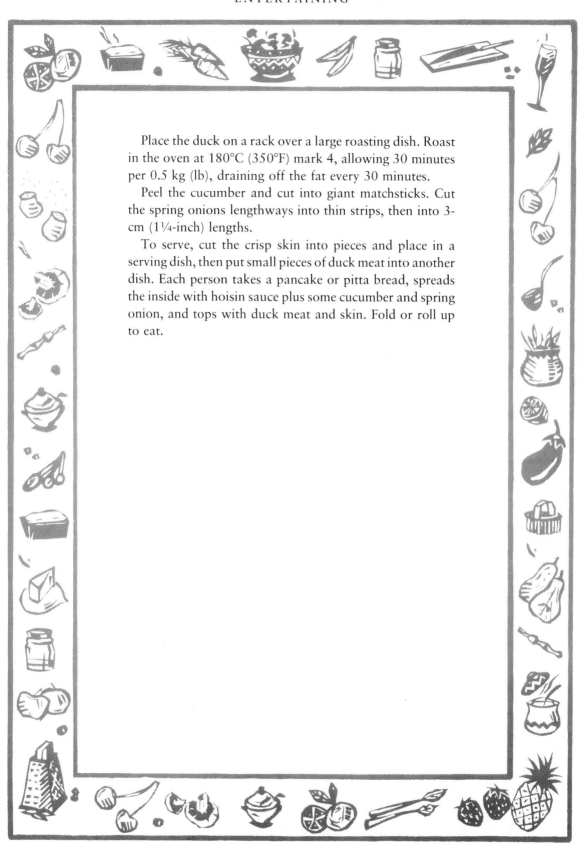

Place the duck on a rack over a large roasting dish. Roast in the oven at 180°C (350°F) mark 4, allowing 30 minutes per 0.5 kg (lb), draining off the fat every 30 minutes.

Peel the cucumber and cut into giant matchsticks. Cut the spring onions lengthways into thin strips, then into 3-cm (1¼-inch) lengths.

To serve, cut the crisp skin into pieces and place in a serving dish, then put small pieces of duck meat into another dish. Each person takes a pancake or pitta bread, spreads the inside with hoisin sauce plus some cucumber and spring onion, and tops with duck meat and skin. Fold or roll up to eat.

Pitta Surprise

356 kcal/1489 kJ
Fat: Low
Fibre: High

*An after-the-film or after-the-match sandwich: you can buy
the egg-fried rice on the way home, or leave some cooked
rice ready chilled to egg-fry in a few minutes when you get
home. Don't leave out the lemon – it adds a tangy touch.
Make this healthier by heating your own rice, rather than
frying it, in a thick-based pan merely brushed with soya
oil, and adding some vitamin C in the form of rings of red
or green pepper or chunks of frilled lettuce. From Cheryl
Painter, Potters Bar.*

TO SERVE 4

225 g (8 oz) chicken, well cooked
soya oil for shallow frying
1 small onion, skinned and sliced
4 large mushrooms, sliced
225 g (8 oz) egg fried rice (see method)
4 pitta bread, warmed
lemon juice

Shred or chop the chicken. Heat a little oil in a pan and
fry the onion and mushrooms until tender, keeping
separate. If using plain cooked rice, heat in oil in a pan,
then scramble 2 beaten eggs with a dash of soy sauce. If
using bought fried rice, heat well. Mix in the fried onions.
Split the pitta bread and put some chicken in the pitta
pockets. Add the rice, fill up with more chicken, squeeze
on some lemon juice and finally add the mushroom slices.

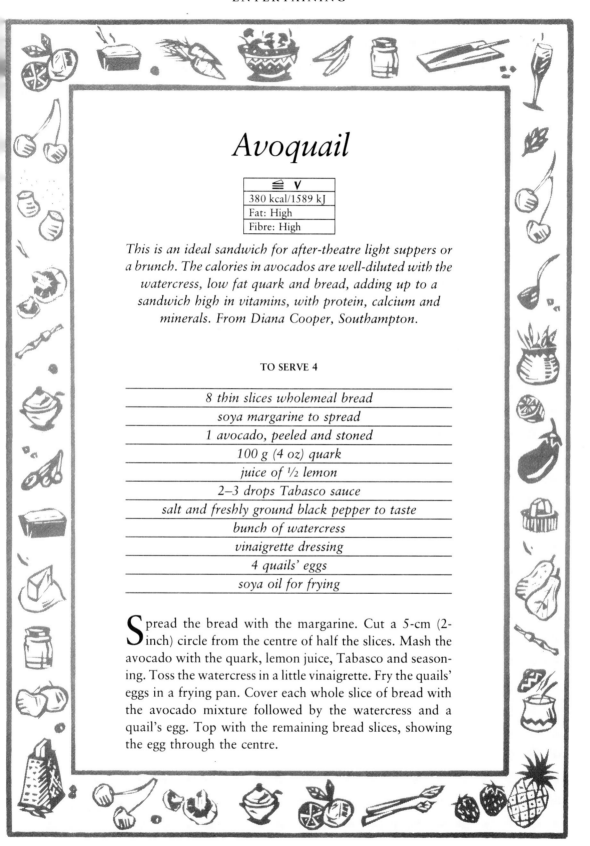

Avoquail

⬳ V
380 kcal/1589 kJ
Fat: High
Fibre: High

This is an ideal sandwich for after-theatre light suppers or a brunch. The calories in avocados are well-diluted with the watercress, low fat quark and bread, adding up to a sandwich high in vitamins, with protein, calcium and minerals. From Diana Cooper, Southampton.

TO SERVE 4

8 thin slices wholemeal bread

soya margarine to spread

1 avocado, peeled and stoned

100 g (4 oz) quark

juice of ½ lemon

2–3 drops Tabasco sauce

salt and freshly ground black pepper to taste

bunch of watercress

vinaigrette dressing

4 quails' eggs

soya oil for frying

Spread the bread with the margarine. Cut a 5-cm (2-inch) circle from the centre of half the slices. Mash the avocado with the quark, lemon juice, Tabasco and seasoning. Toss the watercress in a little vinaigrette. Fry the quails' eggs in a frying pan. Cover each whole slice of bread with the avocado mixture followed by the watercress and a quail's egg. Top with the remaining bread slices, showing the egg through the centre.

Italian Wedgies

⬳ ✿
619 kcal/2588 kJ
Fat: High
Fibre: Medium

*Sensational dish to look at and to eat – a perfect centrepiece
for an informal supper party or picnic, as you can eat it
comfortably with your fingers. Pesto sauce (made with
basil, pine nuts, oil and sometimes Parmesan and garlic) is
available in jars from delicatessens and supermarkets, or is
easily made with fresh basil in a food processor. With
cheese, salami and Mortadella, this is high in saturated fats.
However, it is a good source of B vitamins, with some
calcium from cheese and vitamin C from the tomatoes.
From K Camm, London.*

TO SERVE 6

1 cob loaf or Italian flatbread
soya margarine to spread
45 ml (3 tbsp) pesto sauce
225 g (8 oz) smoked ham, thickly sliced
100 g (4 oz) salami
175 g (6 oz) sliced Mortadella
225 g (8 oz) smoked cheese, sliced
225 g (8 oz) tomatoes, thinly sliced
2.5 ml (½ tsp) sugar
15 ml (1 tbsp) chopped fresh mint
salt and freshly ground black pepper to taste
225 g (8 oz) green olives

→

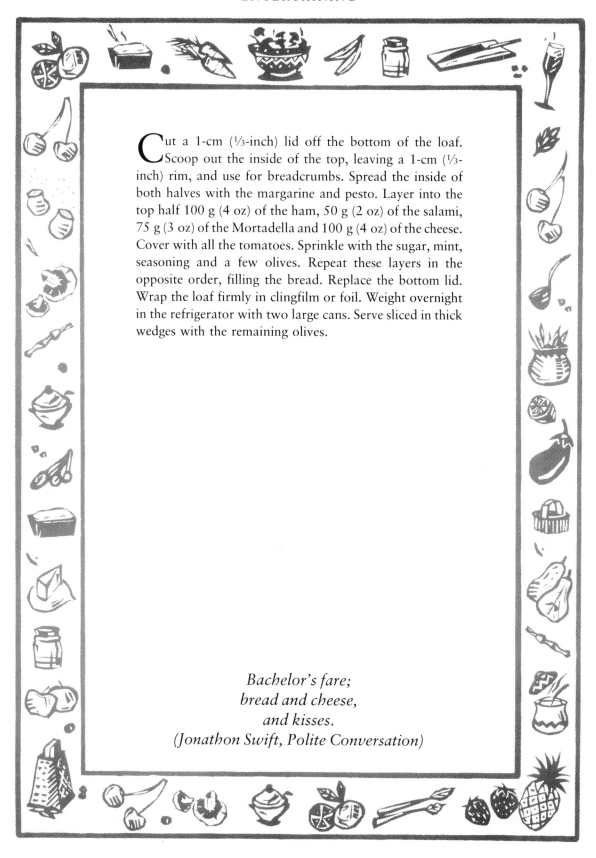

Cut a 1-cm (⅓-inch) lid off the bottom of the loaf. Scoop out the inside of the top, leaving a 1-cm (⅓-inch) rim, and use for breadcrumbs. Spread the inside of both halves with the margarine and pesto. Layer into the top half 100 g (4 oz) of the ham, 50 g (2 oz) of the salami, 75 g (3 oz) of the Mortadella and 100 g (4 oz) of the cheese. Cover with all the tomatoes. Sprinkle with the sugar, mint, seasoning and a few olives. Repeat these layers in the opposite order, filling the bread. Replace the bottom lid. Wrap the loaf firmly in clingfilm or foil. Weight overnight in the refrigerator with two large cans. Serve sliced in thick wedges with the remaining olives.

Bachelor's fare;
bread and cheese,
and kisses.
(Jonathon Swift, Polite Conversation)

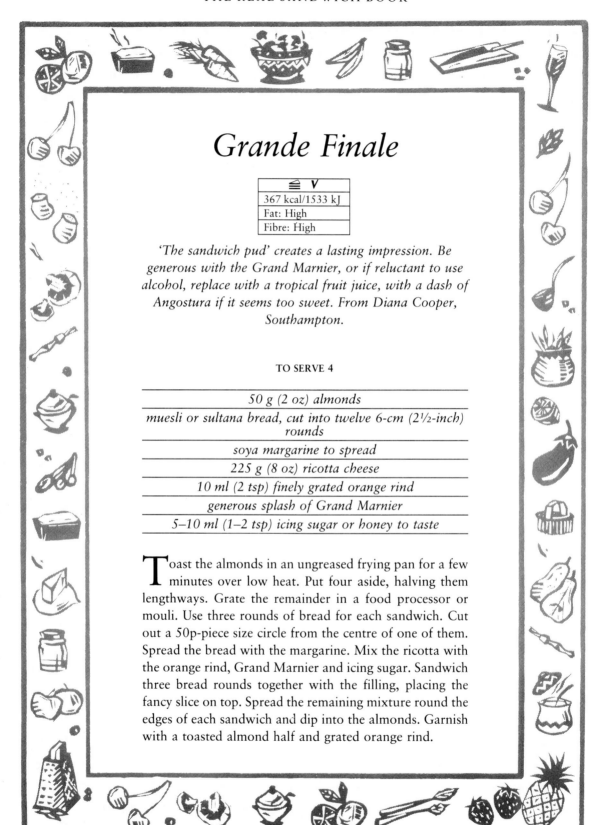

Grande Finale

≙ V
367 kcal/1533 kJ
Fat: High
Fibre: High

'The sandwich pud' creates a lasting impression. Be generous with the Grand Marnier, or if reluctant to use alcohol, replace with a tropical fruit juice, with a dash of Angostura if it seems too sweet. From Diana Cooper, Southampton.

TO SERVE 4

50 g (2 oz) almonds
muesli or sultana bread, cut into twelve 6-cm (2½-inch) rounds
soya margarine to spread
225 g (8 oz) ricotta cheese
10 ml (2 tsp) finely grated orange rind
generous splash of Grand Marnier
5–10 ml (1–2 tsp) icing sugar or honey to taste

Toast the almonds in an ungreased frying pan for a few minutes over low heat. Put four aside, halving them lengthways. Grate the remainder in a food processor or mouli. Use three rounds of bread for each sandwich. Cut out a 50p-piece size circle from the centre of one of them. Spread the bread with the margarine. Mix the ricotta with the orange rind, Grand Marnier and icing sugar. Sandwich three bread rounds together with the filling, placing the fancy slice on top. Spread the remaining mixture round the edges of each sandwich and dip into the almonds. Garnish with a toasted almond half and grated orange rind.

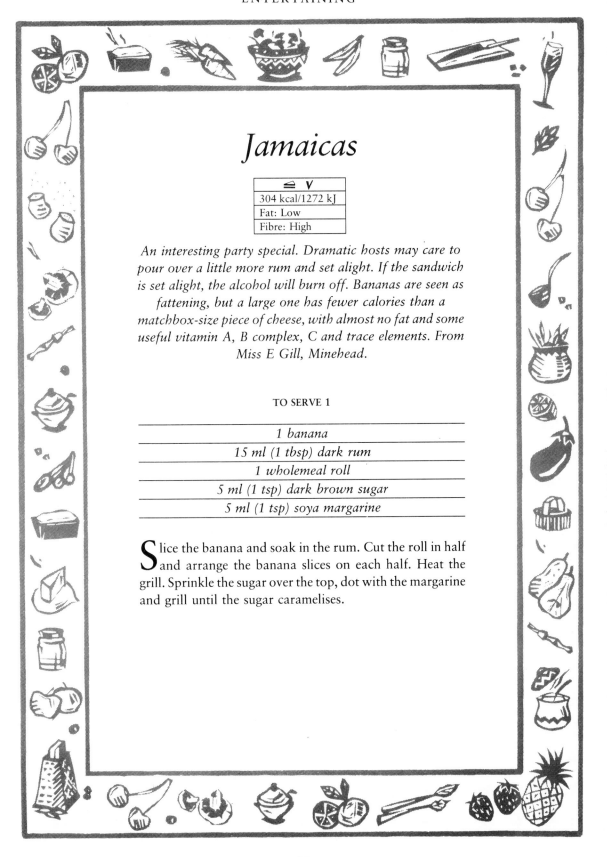

Jamaicas

⇔ V
304 kcal/1272 kJ
Fat: Low
Fibre: High

An interesting party special. Dramatic hosts may care to pour over a little more rum and set alight. If the sandwich is set alight, the alcohol will burn off. Bananas are seen as fattening, but a large one has fewer calories than a matchbox-size piece of cheese, with almost no fat and some useful vitamin A, B complex, C and trace elements. From Miss E Gill, Minehead.

TO SERVE 1

1 banana
15 ml (1 tbsp) dark rum
1 wholemeal roll
5 ml (1 tsp) dark brown sugar
5 ml (1 tsp) soya margarine

Slice the banana and soak in the rum. Cut the roll in half and arrange the banana slices on each half. Heat the grill. Sprinkle the sugar over the top, dot with the margarine and grill until the sugar caramelises.

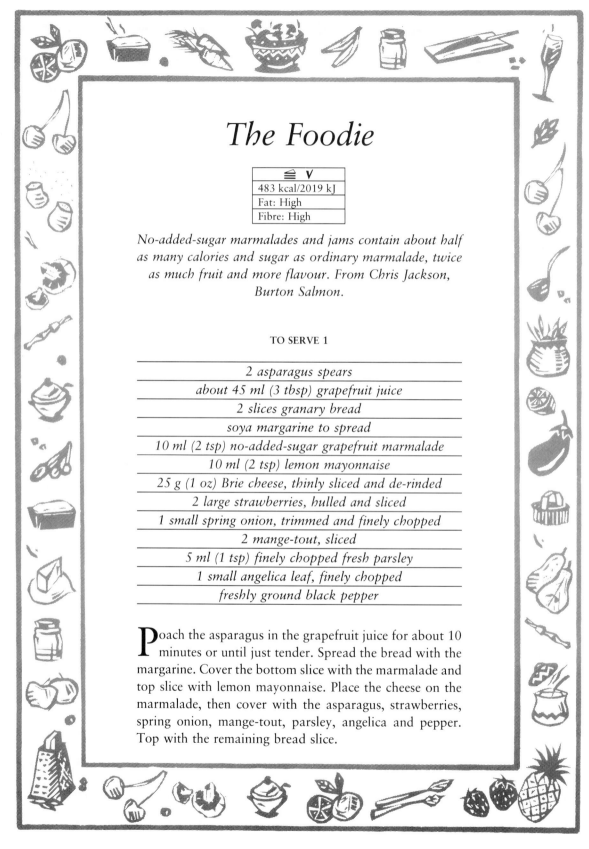

The Foodie

≙ V
483 kcal/2019 kJ
Fat: High
Fibre: High

No-added-sugar marmalades and jams contain about half as many calories and sugar as ordinary marmalade, twice as much fruit and more flavour. From Chris Jackson, Burton Salmon.

TO SERVE 1

2 asparagus spears
about 45 ml (3 tbsp) grapefruit juice
2 slices granary bread
soya margarine to spread
10 ml (2 tsp) no-added-sugar grapefruit marmalade
10 ml (2 tsp) lemon mayonnaise
25 g (1 oz) Brie cheese, thinly sliced and de-rinded
2 large strawberries, hulled and sliced
1 small spring onion, trimmed and finely chopped
2 mange-tout, sliced
5 ml (1 tsp) finely chopped fresh parsley
1 small angelica leaf, finely chopped
freshly ground black pepper

Poach the asparagus in the grapefruit juice for about 10 minutes or until just tender. Spread the bread with the margarine. Cover the bottom slice with the marmalade and top slice with lemon mayonnaise. Place the cheese on the marmalade, then cover with the asparagus, strawberries, spring onion, mange-tout, parsley, angelica and pepper. Top with the remaining bread slice.

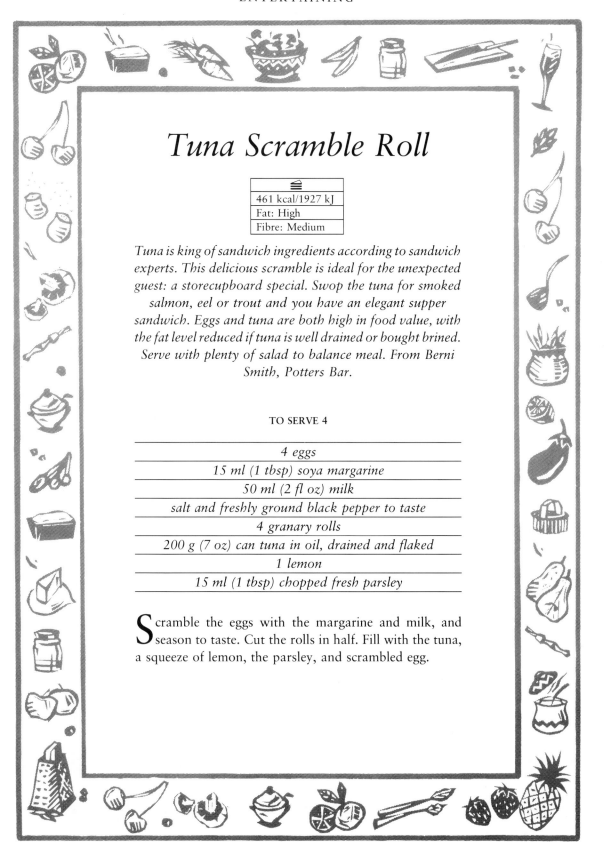

Tuna Scramble Roll

▤
461 kcal/1927 kJ
Fat: High
Fibre: Medium

Tuna is king of sandwich ingredients according to sandwich experts. This delicious scramble is ideal for the unexpected guest: a storecupboard special. Swop the tuna for smoked salmon, eel or trout and you have an elegant supper sandwich. Eggs and tuna are both high in food value, with the fat level reduced if tuna is well drained or bought brined. Serve with plenty of salad to balance meal. From Berni Smith, Potters Bar.

TO SERVE 4

4 eggs
15 ml (1 tbsp) soya margarine
50 ml (2 fl oz) milk
salt and freshly ground black pepper to taste
4 granary rolls
200 g (7 oz) can tuna in oil, drained and flaked
1 lemon
15 ml (1 tbsp) chopped fresh parsley

Scramble the eggs with the margarine and milk, and season to taste. Cut the rolls in half. Fill with the tuna, a squeeze of lemon, the parsley, and scrambled egg.

Smorgasbord

⏪
1158 kcal/4839 kJ
Fat: High
Fibre: Medium

The Scandinavian way with sandwiches seems complicated to prepare, but many of the choices are instant delicatessen items. But try to make at least one speciality yourself, to get the spirit of Scandinavian home entertaining. The joy of smorgasbord is that it gives you such a wide choice of what to serve, and once you've laid everything out, your task as cook is over.

TO SERVE ABOUT 8

2 small loaves of different breads, eg rye bread, white or wholemeal; pumpernickel; caraway seed or poppy seed bread, sliced
pickled herring salad (see recipe)
225 g (8 oz) smoked fish, eg salmon, trout, herring, buckling, eel or a mixture
450 g (1 lb) grav lax (cured marinated salmon) (see recipe)
225 g (8 oz) smoked venison, liver pâté, smoked sausage or ham
225 g (8 oz) shrimps or prawns, freshly cooked
8 eggs, hard-boiled
Swedish meatballs (see recipe)
1 large piece Scandinavian cheese
450 g (1 lb) potato salad
pickled cucumber
1 fresh cucumber and dill salad
soured cream and mustard sauce (see recipe)

Right: Smorgasbord, above

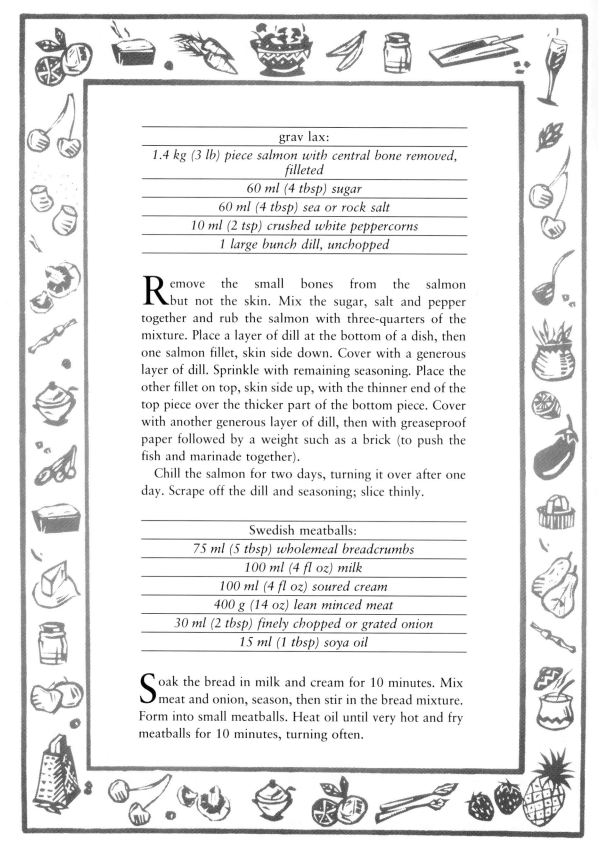

grav lax:
1.4 kg (3 lb) piece salmon with central bone removed, filleted
60 ml (4 tbsp) sugar
60 ml (4 tbsp) sea or rock salt
10 ml (2 tsp) crushed white peppercorns
1 large bunch dill, unchopped

Remove the small bones from the salmon but not the skin. Mix the sugar, salt and pepper together and rub the salmon with three-quarters of the mixture. Place a layer of dill at the bottom of a dish, then one salmon fillet, skin side down. Cover with a generous layer of dill. Sprinkle with remaining seasoning. Place the other fillet on top, skin side up, with the thinner end of the top piece over the thicker part of the bottom piece. Cover with another generous layer of dill, then with greaseproof paper followed by a weight such as a brick (to push the fish and marinade together).

Chill the salmon for two days, turning it over after one day. Scrape off the dill and seasoning; slice thinly.

Swedish meatballs:
75 ml (5 tbsp) wholemeal breadcrumbs
100 ml (4 fl oz) milk
100 ml (4 fl oz) soured cream
400 g (14 oz) lean minced meat
30 ml (2 tbsp) finely chopped or grated onion
15 ml (1 tbsp) soya oil

Soak the bread in milk and cream for 10 minutes. Mix meat and onion, season, then stir in the bread mixture. Form into small meatballs. Heat oil until very hot and fry meatballs for 10 minutes, turning often.

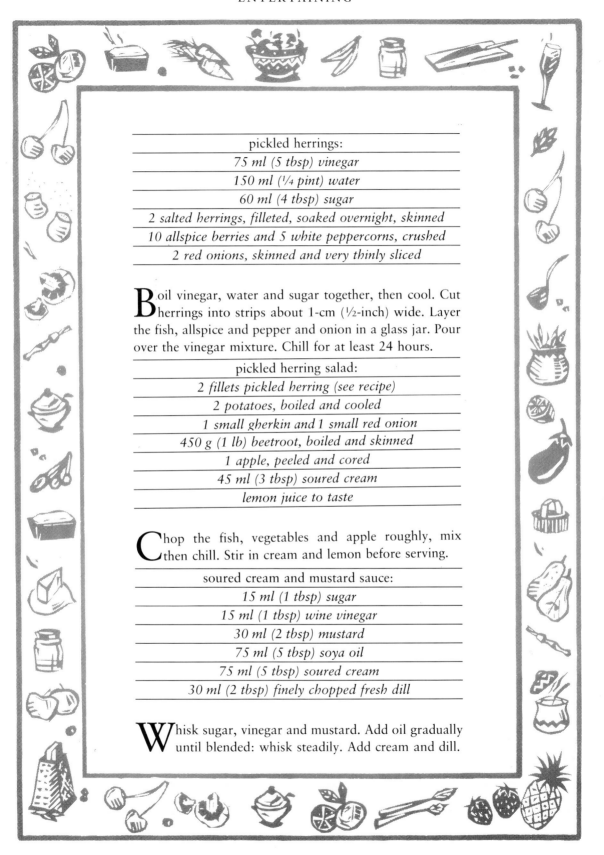

pickled herrings:
75 ml (5 tbsp) vinegar
150 ml (¼ pint) water
60 ml (4 tbsp) sugar
2 salted herrings, filleted, soaked overnight, skinned
10 allspice berries and 5 white peppercorns, crushed
2 red onions, skinned and very thinly sliced

Boil vinegar, water and sugar together, then cool. Cut herrings into strips about 1-cm (½-inch) wide. Layer the fish, allspice and pepper and onion in a glass jar. Pour over the vinegar mixture. Chill for at least 24 hours.

pickled herring salad:
2 fillets pickled herring (see recipe)
2 potatoes, boiled and cooled
1 small gherkin and 1 small red onion
450 g (1 lb) beetroot, boiled and skinned
1 apple, peeled and cored
45 ml (3 tbsp) soured cream
lemon juice to taste

Chop the fish, vegetables and apple roughly, mix then chill. Stir in cream and lemon before serving.

soured cream and mustard sauce:
15 ml (1 tbsp) sugar
15 ml (1 tbsp) wine vinegar
30 ml (2 tbsp) mustard
75 ml (5 tbsp) soya oil
75 ml (5 tbsp) soured cream
30 ml (2 tbsp) finely chopped fresh dill

Whisk sugar, vinegar and mustard. Add oil gradually until blended: whisk steadily. Add cream and dill.

Lunchbox Sandwiches

A lunchbox sandwich has a tight job specification. It must not distintegrate nor leak on the way to work or school. It must be sufficiently neat-to-eat that it can be consumed in a public place without causing embarrassment. It must refresh and fortify without laying you out for half the afternoon. It must be satisfying enough that you don't go on to fill yourself up with cakes and chocolates. Our selection is guaranteed to satisfy all these criteria.

Top lunchbox ingredients

First choice for lunchbox eating is soft cheese, because of its ability to hold ingredients together while travelling or eating. Full fat soft cheese can be 45% fat, mainly saturated, but a huge variety of alternatives offer everything from 1 to 15% fat. The very low fat products tend to leak water and dry out, so go for something around 7% fat (fromage frais or some quark) or up to 12% (medium fat curd cheese). Soft cheese mates perfectly with savoury or sweet fillings, controlling items which are otherwise unruly, such as finely chopped celery, carrot or cucumber. It brings out the flavour of items like banana or mushrooms and its melting smoothness is a good contrast to crunchy ingredients like toasted nuts or crisp bacon.

Alternatives for the same job are peanut butter and mashed banana. To keep bananas, avocados, apples or pears from browning in transit, a squeeze of fresh lemon (or orange) juice is far better-tasting than bottled. If sandwiches with none of the binding talents above are used, the temptation is to lay on mayonnaise. But weightwatchers are aware that even a modest dollop adds over 100 calories to your sandwich.

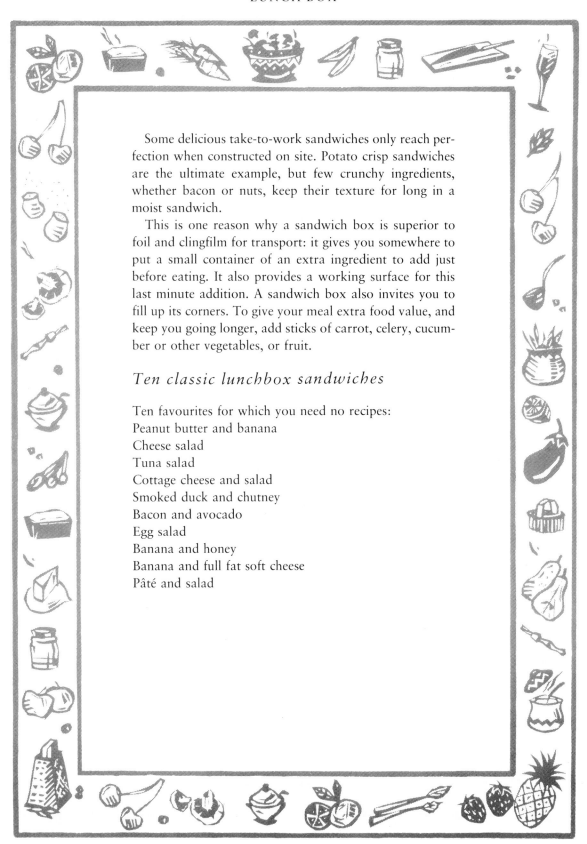

Some delicious take-to-work sandwiches only reach perfection when constructed on site. Potato crisp sandwiches are the ultimate example, but few crunchy ingredients, whether bacon or nuts, keep their texture for long in a moist sandwich.

This is one reason why a sandwich box is superior to foil and clingfilm for transport: it gives you somewhere to put a small container of an extra ingredient to add just before eating. It also provides a working surface for this last minute addition. A sandwich box also invites you to fill up its corners. To give your meal extra food value, and keep you going longer, add sticks of carrot, celery, cucumber or other vegetables, or fruit.

Ten classic lunchbox sandwiches

Ten favourites for which you need no recipes:
Peanut butter and banana
Cheese salad
Tuna salad
Cottage cheese and salad
Smoked duck and chutney
Bacon and avocado
Egg salad
Banana and honey
Banana and full fat soft cheese
Pâté and salad

Afficionado's Crisp Butty

⌐ V
675 kcal/2821 kJ
Fat: Medium
Fibre: High

The critical feature of a crisp butty is that it must be made only just before eating to avoid sogginess. You need only prepare the bread before work. Adults as well as children eat these sandwiches. Crisps average 36% fat, and although the quantity eaten is not heavy, this dish adds up to about 25 g (1 oz) fat from crisps alone per head. Although fried in vegetable fat, some of it is saturated, so though not wildly wicked, not a sandwich for daily use. Crisps provide a little vitamin C, but try adding some tomatoes or other salad.
From Michael Hall, Stainbeck High School.

TO SERVE 2

8 slices soft grain bread
soya margarine to spread
1 packet salt and vinegar crisps
1 packet cheese and onion crisps
1 packet prawn cocktail crisps
tomato ketchup (optional)

Spread the bread with the margarine. Cover two slices of bread with salt and vinegar crisps. Add a second bread slice to each sandwich and cover with cheese and onion crisps. Top with another two slices of bread and add prawn cocktail crisps to these. Press on the final two slices of bread. Ketchup is optional at any stage.

Blue Heaven

≙ ⚙ V
413 kcal/1727 kJ
Fat: High
Fibre: High

A working lunch winner: luxurious to eat, yet fresh, not so heavy that it knocks you out for the afternoon, and easy to make. For a sandwich that will really keep you going use rye pumpernickel; for a neater eat, choose ordinary rye, cutting the slices as large as possible. Cucumber, celery and carrot turn this into a salad meal, providing vitamins A (and C in modest amounts), plus useful B vitamins from the bread, cheese and walnuts, and fibre from the bread and walnuts – a good package. From Helena Thomas, Wroughton, Wiltshire.

TO SERVE 1

2 slices rye bread
soya margarine to spread
5-cm (2-inch) piece cucumber
15 ml (1 tbsp) natural yogurt
25 g (1 oz) blue cheese
1 stick celery, finely chopped
1 carrot, peeled and grated
25 g (1 oz) walnut pieces, finely chopped
freshly ground black pepper to taste

Spread the bread with the margarine. Grate the cucumber and mash with the yogurt and blue cheese. Mix in the remaining ingredients, adding pepper to taste. Cover one slice of bread with the filling, then top with the remaining bread slice.

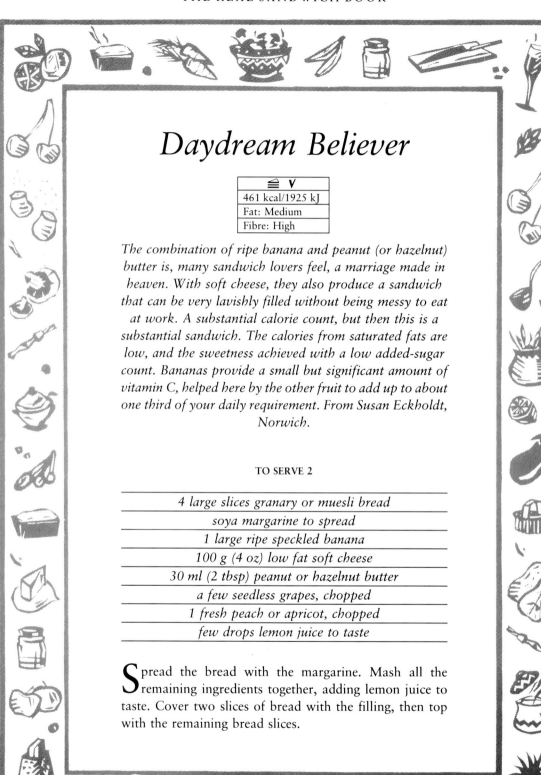

Daydream Believer

⊜ V
461 kcal/1925 kJ
Fat: Medium
Fibre: High

The combination of ripe banana and peanut (or hazelnut) butter is, many sandwich lovers feel, a marriage made in heaven. With soft cheese, they also produce a sandwich that can be very lavishly filled without being messy to eat at work. A substantial calorie count, but then this is a substantial sandwich. The calories from saturated fats are low, and the sweetness achieved with a low added-sugar count. Bananas provide a small but significant amount of vitamin C, helped here by the other fruit to add up to about one third of your daily requirement. From Susan Eckholdt, Norwich.

TO SERVE 2

4 large slices granary or muesli bread

soya margarine to spread

1 large ripe speckled banana

100 g (4 oz) low fat soft cheese

30 ml (2 tbsp) peanut or hazelnut butter

a few seedless grapes, chopped

1 fresh peach or apricot, chopped

few drops lemon juice to taste

Spread the bread with the margarine. Mash all the remaining ingredients together, adding lemon juice to taste. Cover two slices of bread with the filling, then top with the remaining bread slices.

Pine Parcel

⌒ V	
476 kcal/1991 kJ	
Fat: High	
Fibre: Medium	

Invented with a dual purpose, this parcelled-up filling keeps the sandwich contents a surprise when you make them for others, and makes the sandwich neat to eat. Avoid blandness by toasting the pine kernels briefly in an ungreased frying pan to bring out the flavour, and by seasoning mixture generously. Full fat soft cheese can be almost as much as half fat, mainly saturated. However, this sandwich is easily improved by using a smooth low fat cheese. Pine kernels are high in oil (about 150 calories per 25 g (1 oz)) and also in useful fatty acids. Make very sure those you use are fresh and sweet-tasting, not unhealthily rancid. From Ann Morris, Leeds.

TO SERVE 1

1 round crusty roll
soya margarine to spread
15 ml (1 tbsp) pine kernels
50 g (2 oz) full fat soft cheese
1 large soft lettuce leaf

Slice the top off the roll about one third of the way down. Scoop out the bread from the bottom of the roll, then spread the inside and the top of the roll with the margarine. Toast the pine kernels in an ungreased frying pan over low heat for about 1 minute. Mix the pine kernels and cheese together, wrap in the lettuce leaf to make a parcel. Put the parcel in the bottom of the roll, then replace the top.

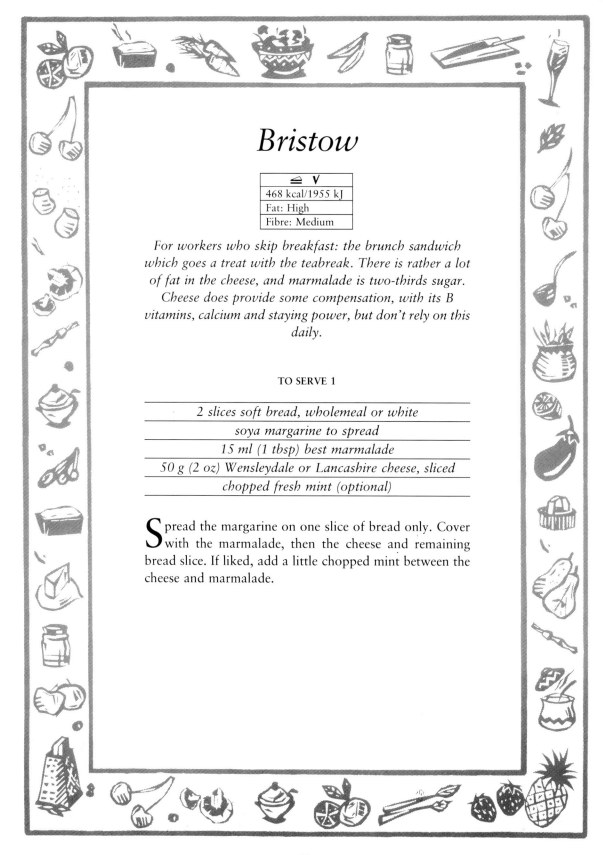

Bristow

⬅ V
468 kcal/1955 kJ
Fat: High
Fibre: Medium

For workers who skip breakfast: the brunch sandwich which goes a treat with the teabreak. There is rather a lot of fat in the cheese, and marmalade is two-thirds sugar. Cheese does provide some compensation, with its B vitamins, calcium and staying power, but don't rely on this daily.

TO SERVE 1

2 slices soft bread, wholemeal or white
soya margarine to spread
15 ml (1 tbsp) best marmalade
50 g (2 oz) Wensleydale or Lancashire cheese, sliced
chopped fresh mint (optional)

Spread the margarine on one slice of bread only. Cover with the marmalade, then the cheese and remaining bread slice. If liked, add a little chopped mint between the cheese and marmalade.

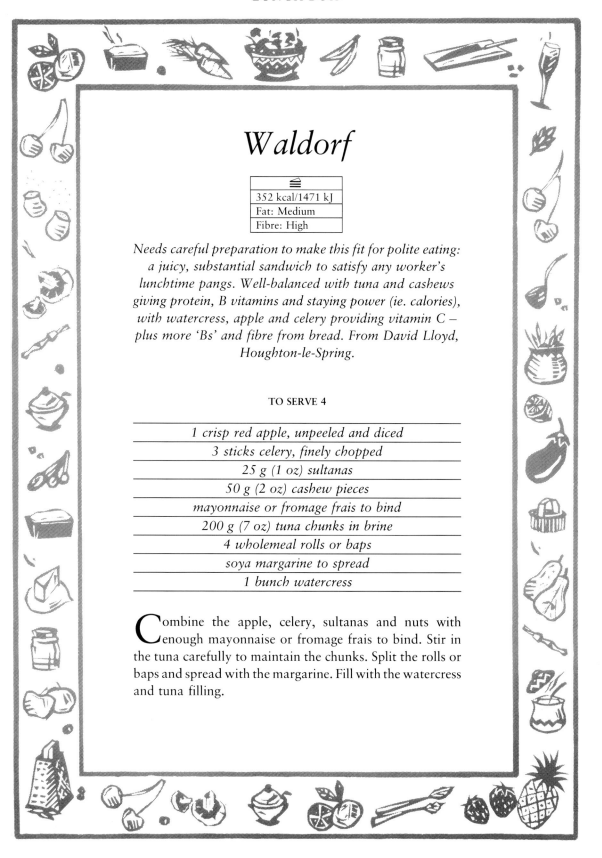

Waldorf

⬃
352 kcal/1471 kJ
Fat: Medium
Fibre: High

Needs careful preparation to make this fit for polite eating: a juicy, substantial sandwich to satisfy any worker's lunchtime pangs. Well-balanced with tuna and cashews giving protein, B vitamins and staying power (ie. calories), with watercress, apple and celery providing vitamin C – plus more 'Bs' and fibre from bread. From David Lloyd, Houghton-le-Spring.

TO SERVE 4

1 crisp red apple, unpeeled and diced
3 sticks celery, finely chopped
25 g (1 oz) sultanas
50 g (2 oz) cashew pieces
mayonnaise or fromage frais to bind
200 g (7 oz) tuna chunks in brine
4 wholemeal rolls or baps
soya margarine to spread
1 bunch watercress

Combine the apple, celery, sultanas and nuts with enough mayonnaise or fromage frais to bind. Stir in the tuna carefully to maintain the chunks. Split the rolls or baps and spread with the margarine. Fill with the watercress and tuna filling.

Hangover Cure

⌂
653 kcal/2731 kJ
Fat: High
Fibre: Medium

It may seem antisocial to suggest a sandwich incorporating garlic and leek for the workplace, but there are times when strong measures are needed, and the onion family is famous for clearing the bloodstream and head, coupled with circulation-boosting radishes and pepper. Grill bacon thoroughly to drain off as much fat as possible – but quite a lot will stay, giving this sandwich a not-for-everyday tag. The green parts of leeks are an excellent source of vitamin C. From K Camm, London.

TO SERVE 1

2 slices mixed grain bread
soya margarine to spread
10 ml (2 tsp) garlic mayonnaise
4 rashers smoked streaky bacon
15 ml (1 tbsp) thinly sliced young leeks
2 radishes, thinly sliced
freshly ground black pepper

Spread the bread with the margarine and mayonnaise. Mix the remaining ingredients together. Cover one slice of bread with the filling, then top with the remaining bread slice.

Right: Waldorf (*right*), page 73 and Blue Heaven (*left*), page 69

Squirrel Nutkin

≙ V		
519 kcal/2169 kJ		
Fat: High		
Fibre: High		

A fresh-tasting lunchtime treat. The baton is important, as it gives the sandwich enough substance to keep you away from supplementary stodge. Not low in calories, because of the hazelnuts, though these are much lower, at about 107 per 25 g (1 oz) than the average 150 for other nuts. This sandwich has both high vitamin and mineral content.
From Valerie Garner, Leicester.

TO SERVE 1

50 g (2 oz) hazelnuts
soya margarine to spread
1 small granary baton
50 g (2 oz) mushrooms, finely sliced
100 g (4 oz) cottage cheese
15 ml (1 tbsp) reduced calorie salad cream
freshly ground black pepper to taste
a few young dandelion leaves and handful of watercress to garnish

Toast the hazelnuts in an ungreased frying pan over low heat for a few minutes, shaking the pan occasionally to turn them. Grate or grind half of them and mix with the margarine. Split the baton and spread with the nut margarine. Finely slice the remaining nuts and mix with the mushrooms, cottage cheese, salad cream and pepper. Pile on to the baton. Garnish with the dandelion and watercress.

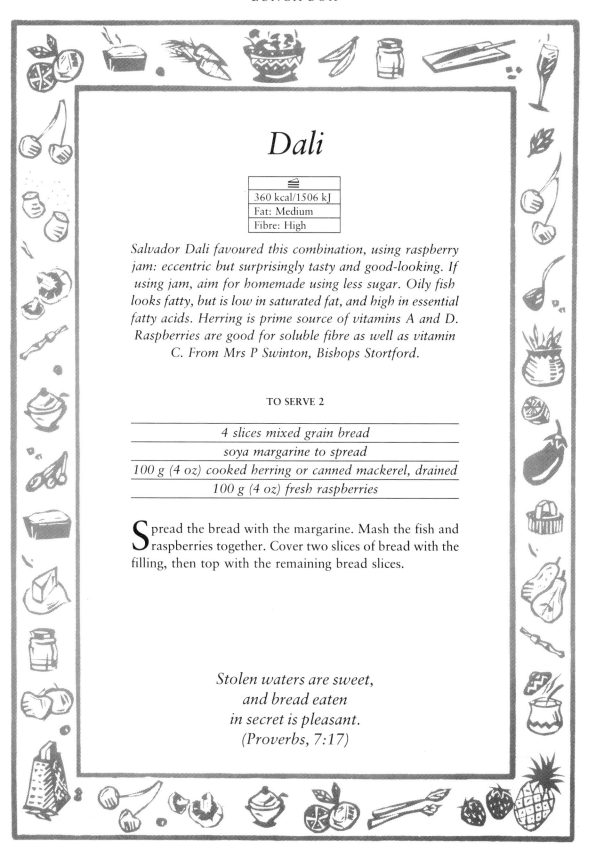

Dali

360 kcal/1506 kJ
Fat: Medium
Fibre: High

Salvador Dali favoured this combination, using raspberry jam: eccentric but surprisingly tasty and good-looking. If using jam, aim for homemade using less sugar. Oily fish looks fatty, but is low in saturated fat, and high in essential fatty acids. Herring is prime source of vitamins A and D. Raspberries are good for soluble fibre as well as vitamin C. From Mrs P Swinton, Bishops Stortford.

TO SERVE 2

4 slices mixed grain bread

soya margarine to spread

100 g (4 oz) cooked herring or canned mackerel, drained

100 g (4 oz) fresh raspberries

Spread the bread with the margarine. Mash the fish and raspberries together. Cover two slices of bread with the filling, then top with the remaining bread slices.

Stolen waters are sweet,
and bread eaten
in secret is pleasant.
(Proverbs, 7:17)

Helsinkis

⬓
439 kcal/1837 kJ
Fat: Medium
Fibre: High

Dill is the key flavouring of Scandinavian food: a fresh, clean flavour that goes beautifully with fish, eggs and salad. Build them all into a substantial picnic. Grav lax is well worth making: a salmon piece is often a bargain, and grav lax makes it go a long way, luxuriously. In spite of the soured cream (18% fat – far less than full fat soft cheese), this is a high nutrition sandwich, with reasonably low fat, but plenty of B vitamins, some useful essential fatty acids and vitamins A and D. Top up with vitamin C with a side salad.

TO SERVE 2

200 g (7 oz) kipper fillet or grav lax (see page 64)
30 ml (2 tbsp) soured cream
about 5 ml (1 tsp) wholegrain mustard to taste
freshly ground black pepper
5 ml (1 tsp) chopped fresh dill (optional)
4 slices mixed grain bread
10-cm (4-inch) piece cucumber, thinly sliced
1 egg, hard-boiled

Mash the kipper with the soured cream, mustard, pepper and dill, if using. Cover each slice of bread with a thin layer of cucumber slices, then with the kipper mixture. Serve as open sandwiches, garnished with egg slices and a little extra dill or cucumber.

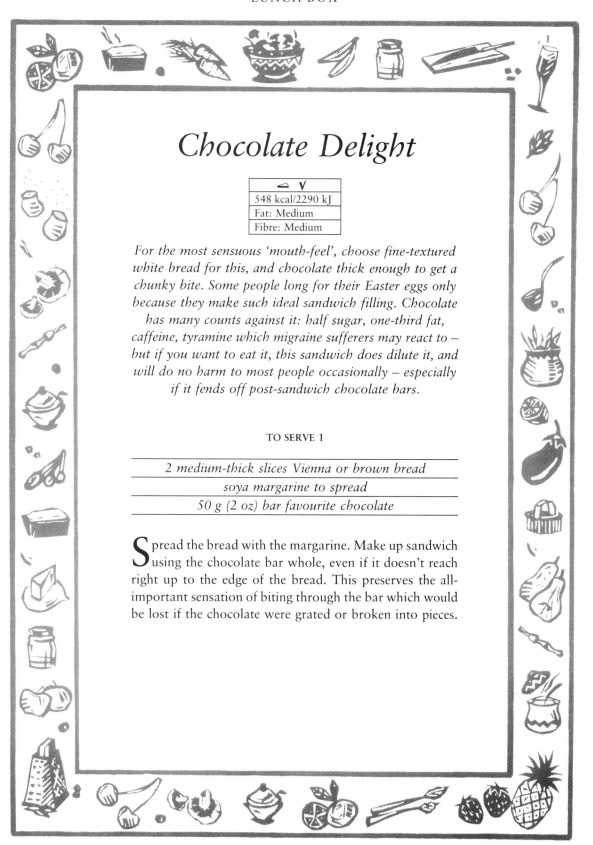

Chocolate Delight

⏤ V		
548 kcal/2290 kJ		
Fat: Medium		
Fibre: Medium		

For the most sensuous 'mouth-feel', choose fine-textured white bread for this, and chocolate thick enough to get a chunky bite. Some people long for their Easter eggs only because they make such ideal sandwich filling. Chocolate has many counts against it: half sugar, one-third fat, caffeine, tyramine which migraine sufferers may react to – but if you want to eat it, this sandwich does dilute it, and will do no harm to most people occasionally – especially if it fends off post-sandwich chocolate bars.

TO SERVE 1

2 medium-thick slices Vienna or brown bread

soya margarine to spread

50 g (2 oz) bar favourite chocolate

Spread the bread with the margarine. Make up sandwich using the chocolate bar whole, even if it doesn't reach right up to the edge of the bread. This preserves the all-important sensation of biting through the bar which would be lost if the chocolate were grated or broken into pieces.

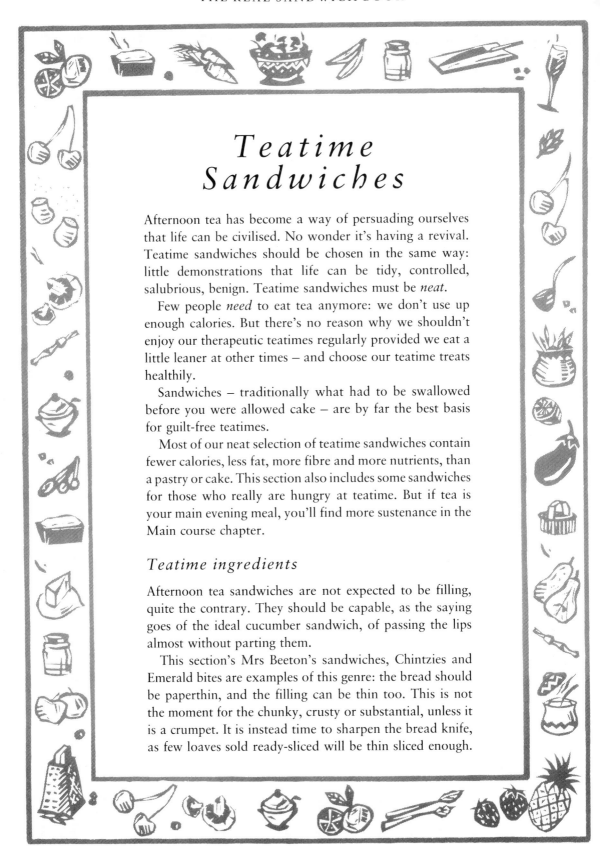

Teatime Sandwiches

Afternoon tea has become a way of persuading ourselves that life can be civilised. No wonder it's having a revival. Teatime sandwiches should be chosen in the same way: little demonstrations that life can be tidy, controlled, salubrious, benign. Teatime sandwiches must be *neat*.

Few people *need* to eat tea anymore: we don't use up enough calories. But there's no reason why we shouldn't enjoy our therapeutic teatimes regularly provided we eat a little leaner at other times – and choose our teatime treats healthily.

Sandwiches – traditionally what had to be swallowed before you were allowed cake – are by far the best basis for guilt-free teatimes.

Most of our neat selection of teatime sandwiches contain fewer calories, less fat, more fibre and more nutrients, than a pastry or cake. This section also includes some sandwiches for those who really are hungry at teatime. But if tea is your main evening meal, you'll find more sustenance in the Main course chapter.

Teatime ingredients

Afternoon tea sandwiches are not expected to be filling, quite the contrary. They should be capable, as the saying goes of the ideal cucumber sandwich, of passing the lips almost without parting them.

This section's Mrs Beeton's sandwiches, Chintzies and Emerald bites are examples of this genre: the bread should be paperthin, and the filling can be thin too. This is not the moment for the chunky, crusty or substantial, unless it is a crumpet. It is instead time to sharpen the bread knife, as few loaves sold ready-sliced will be thin sliced enough.

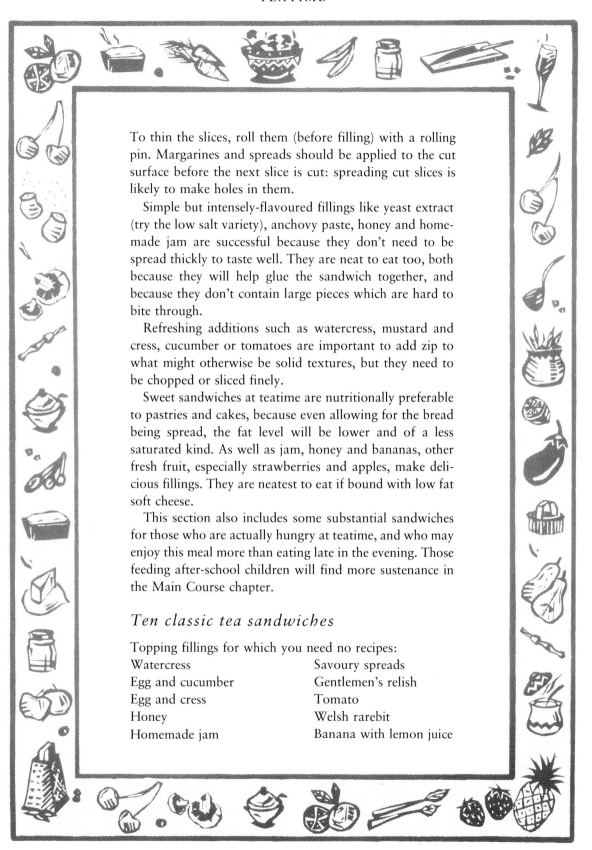

To thin the slices, roll them (before filling) with a rolling pin. Margarines and spreads should be applied to the cut surface before the next slice is cut: spreading cut slices is likely to make holes in them.

Simple but intensely-flavoured fillings like yeast extract (try the low salt variety), anchovy paste, honey and home-made jam are successful because they don't need to be spread thickly to taste well. They are neat to eat too, both because they will help glue the sandwich together, and because they don't contain large pieces which are hard to bite through.

Refreshing additions such as watercress, mustard and cress, cucumber or tomatoes are important to add zip to what might otherwise be solid textures, but they need to be chopped or sliced finely.

Sweet sandwiches at teatime are nutritionally preferable to pastries and cakes, because even allowing for the bread being spread, the fat level will be lower and of a less saturated kind. As well as jam, honey and bananas, other fresh fruit, especially strawberries and apples, make delicious fillings. They are neatest to eat if bound with low fat soft cheese.

This section also includes some substantial sandwiches for those who are actually hungry at teatime, and who may enjoy this meal more than eating late in the evening. Those feeding after-school children will find more sustenance in the Main Course chapter.

Ten classic tea sandwiches

Topping fillings for which you need no recipes:

Watercress	Savoury spreads
Egg and cucumber	Gentlemen's relish
Egg and cress	Tomato
Honey	Welsh rarebit
Homemade jam	Banana with lemon juice

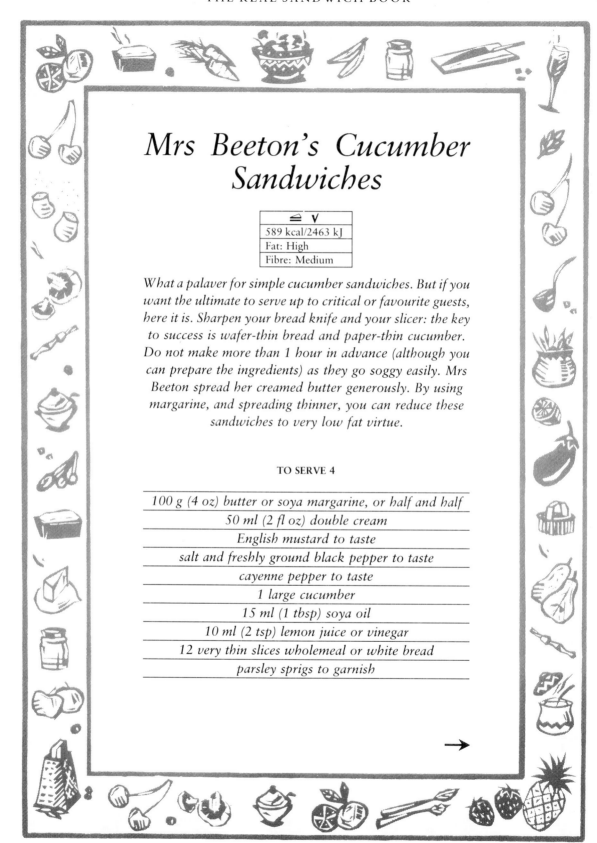

Mrs Beeton's Cucumber Sandwiches

≙	V
589 kcal/2463 kJ	
Fat: High	
Fibre: Medium	

What a palaver for simple cucumber sandwiches. But if you want the ultimate to serve up to critical or favourite guests, here it is. Sharpen your bread knife and your slicer: the key to success is wafer-thin bread and paper-thin cucumber. Do not make more than 1 hour in advance (although you can prepare the ingredients) as they go soggy easily. Mrs Beeton spread her creamed butter generously. By using margarine, and spreading thinner, you can reduce these sandwiches to very low fat virtue.

TO SERVE 4

100 g (4 oz) butter or soya margarine, or half and half

50 ml (2 fl oz) double cream

English mustard to taste

salt and freshly ground black pepper to taste

cayenne pepper to taste

1 large cucumber

15 ml (1 tbsp) soya oil

10 ml (2 tsp) lemon juice or vinegar

12 very thin slices wholemeal or white bread

parsley sprigs to garnish

→

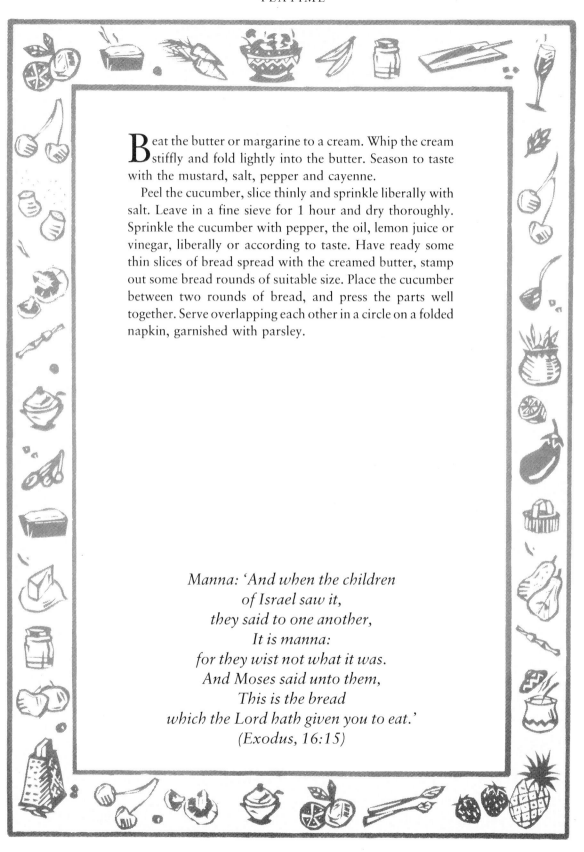

Beat the butter or margarine to a cream. Whip the cream stiffly and fold lightly into the butter. Season to taste with the mustard, salt, pepper and cayenne.

Peel the cucumber, slice thinly and sprinkle liberally with salt. Leave in a fine sieve for 1 hour and dry thoroughly. Sprinkle the cucumber with pepper, the oil, lemon juice or vinegar, liberally or according to taste. Have ready some thin slices of bread spread with the creamed butter, stamp out some bread rounds of suitable size. Place the cucumber between two rounds of bread, and press the parts well together. Serve overlapping each other in a circle on a folded napkin, garnished with parsley.

Manna: 'And when the children
of Israel saw it,
they said to one another,
It is manna:
for they wist not what it was.
And Moses said unto them,
This is the bread
which the Lord hath given you to eat.'
(Exodus, 16:15)

Blue Rondo

⊿ V
344 kcal/1438 kJ
Fat: High
Fibre: High

*The fourth 'blue' in this book – and everyone a winner.
Stilton is one of the highest fat cheeses at around 30% fat.
If you want to enjoy this sandwich more often, use 15 g
(½ oz) Stilton blended with 25 g (1 oz) low fat soft cheese
or quark. From Lisa Green, Sheffield.*

TO SERVE 1

1 soft grain crumpet
soya margarine to spread
½ pear, sliced
juice of ½ lemon
freshly ground black pepper
15 g (½ oz) walnuts, chopped
40 g (1½ oz) Stilton cheese, crumbled
1 walnut half to garnish

Toast the crumpet base. Spread the top with the margarine. Cover with the pear and sprinkle with lemon juice. Top with the pepper, nuts, then the Stilton. Grill until the cheese is golden brown and bubbling. Garnish with the walnut half.

Norland Fancy

 V
227 kcal/948 kJ
Fat: Medium
Fibre: High

Favoured by nannies as a neat eat for messy toddlers but really because they love them, these go down a treat at any form of tea party, so make about twice as many as you think you need. Also delicious substituting chopped crystallised ginger for 25 g (1 oz) of the dates. A combination of bread and cheese give these sandwiches plenty of protein and B vitamins. Natural partners with any kind of fruit from pineapple to blackberries which provide vitamins A and C. From Liz Davies, Kingston-on-Thames.

TO SERVE 4

6 slices wholemeal or malt bread

soya margarine to spread

100 g (4 oz) low fat soft cheese

50 g (2 oz) dates, stoned and chopped

ground cinnamon to taste

Spread the bread with the margarine. Mash the soft cheese with the dates and cinnamon to taste. Spread the filling on to three slices of bread. Top with the remaining bread slices and cut into small neat shapes.

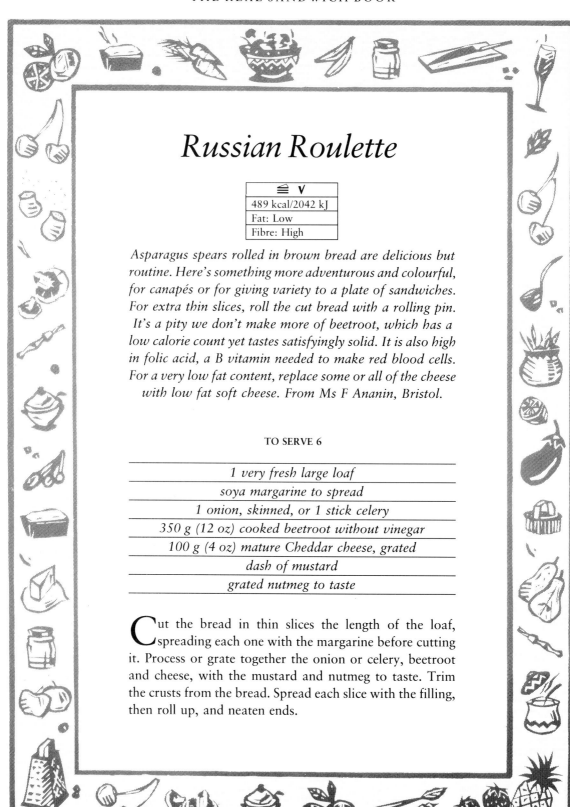

Russian Roulette

≙ v
489 kcal/2042 kJ
Fat: Low
Fibre: High

Asparagus spears rolled in brown bread are delicious but routine. Here's something more adventurous and colourful, for canapés or for giving variety to a plate of sandwiches. For extra thin slices, roll the cut bread with a rolling pin. It's a pity we don't make more of beetroot, which has a low calorie count yet tastes satisfyingly solid. It is also high in folic acid, a B vitamin needed to make red blood cells. For a very low fat content, replace some or all of the cheese with low fat soft cheese. From Ms F Ananin, Bristol.

TO SERVE 6

1 very fresh large loaf

soya margarine to spread

1 onion, skinned, or 1 stick celery

350 g (12 oz) cooked beetroot without vinegar

100 g (4 oz) mature Cheddar cheese, grated

dash of mustard

grated nutmeg to taste

Cut the bread in thin slices the length of the loaf, spreading each one with the margarine before cutting it. Process or grate together the onion or celery, beetroot and cheese, with the mustard and nutmeg to taste. Trim the crusts from the bread. Spread each slice with the filling, then roll up, and neaten ends.

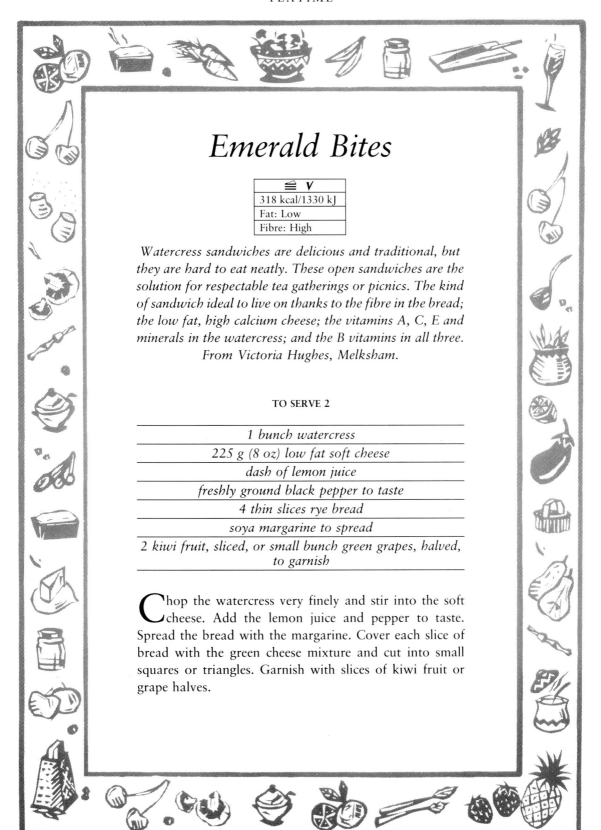

Emerald Bites

≣ V
318 kcal/1330 kJ
Fat: Low
Fibre: High

Watercress sandwiches are delicious and traditional, but they are hard to eat neatly. These open sandwiches are the solution for respectable tea gatherings or picnics. The kind of sandwich ideal to live on thanks to the fibre in the bread; the low fat, high calcium cheese; the vitamins A, C, E and minerals in the watercress; and the B vitamins in all three.
From Victoria Hughes, Melksham.

TO SERVE 2

1 bunch watercress
225 g (8 oz) low fat soft cheese
dash of lemon juice
freshly ground black pepper to taste
4 thin slices rye bread
soya margarine to spread
2 kiwi fruit, sliced, or small bunch green grapes, halved, to garnish

Chop the watercress very finely and stir into the soft cheese. Add the lemon juice and pepper to taste. Spread the bread with the margarine. Cover each slice of bread with the green cheese mixture and cut into small squares or triangles. Garnish with slices of kiwi fruit or grape halves.

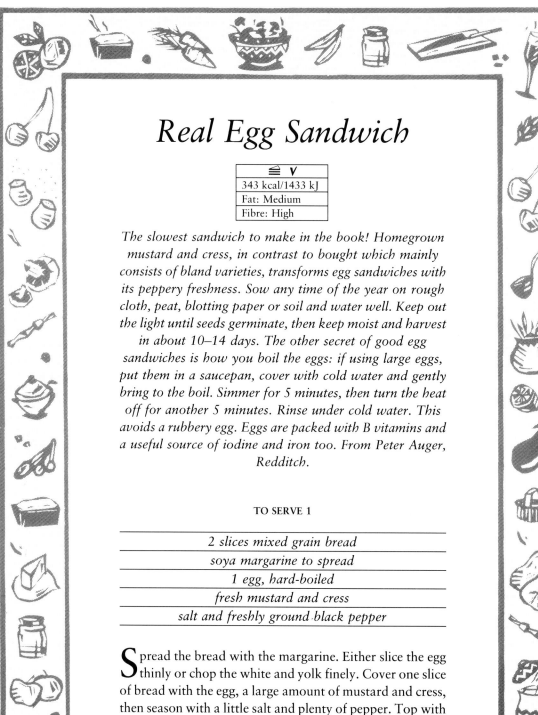

Real Egg Sandwich

≘ v
343 kcal/1433 kJ
Fat: Medium
Fibre: High

The slowest sandwich to make in the book! Homegrown mustard and cress, in contrast to bought which mainly consists of bland varieties, transforms egg sandwiches with its peppery freshness. Sow any time of the year on rough cloth, peat, blotting paper or soil and water well. Keep out the light until seeds germinate, then keep moist and harvest in about 10–14 days. The other secret of good egg sandwiches is how you boil the eggs: if using large eggs, put them in a saucepan, cover with cold water and gently bring to the boil. Simmer for 5 minutes, then turn the heat off for another 5 minutes. Rinse under cold water. This avoids a rubbery egg. Eggs are packed with B vitamins and a useful source of iodine and iron too. From Peter Auger, Redditch.

TO SERVE 1

2 slices mixed grain bread

soya margarine to spread

1 egg, hard-boiled

fresh mustard and cress

salt and freshly ground black pepper

Spread the bread with the margarine. Either slice the egg thinly or chop the white and yolk finely. Cover one slice of bread with the egg, a large amount of mustard and cress, then season with a little salt and plenty of pepper. Top with the remaining bread slice.

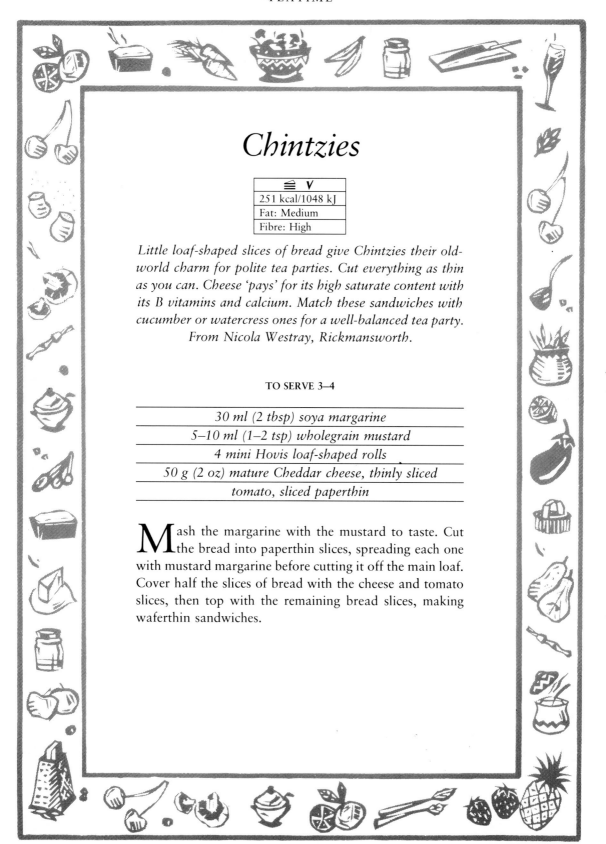

Chintzies

≧ v
251 kcal/1048 kJ
Fat: Medium
Fibre: High

Little loaf-shaped slices of bread give Chintzies their old-world charm for polite tea parties. Cut everything as thin as you can. Cheese 'pays' for its high saturate content with its B vitamins and calcium. Match these sandwiches with cucumber or watercress ones for a well-balanced tea party. From Nicola Westray, Rickmansworth.

TO SERVE 3–4

30 ml (2 tbsp) soya margarine

5–10 ml (1–2 tsp) wholegrain mustard

4 mini Hovis loaf-shaped rolls

50 g (2 oz) mature Cheddar cheese, thinly sliced

tomato, sliced paperthin

Mash the margarine with the mustard to taste. Cut the bread into paperthin slices, spreading each one with mustard margarine before cutting it off the main loaf. Cover half the slices of bread with the cheese and tomato slices, then top with the remaining bread slices, making waferthin sandwiches.

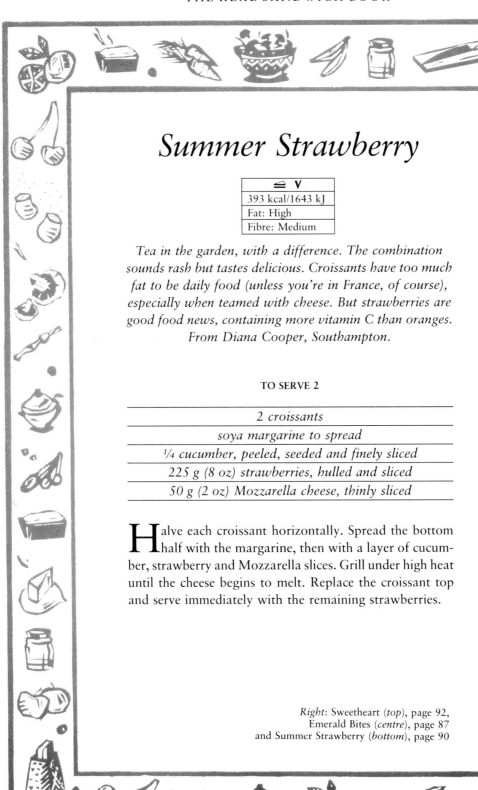

Summer Strawberry

≜ V
393 kcal/1643 kJ
Fat: High
Fibre: Medium

Tea in the garden, with a difference. The combination sounds rash but tastes delicious. Croissants have too much fat to be daily food (unless you're in France, of course), especially when teamed with cheese. But strawberries are good food news, containing more vitamin C than oranges. From Diana Cooper, Southampton.

TO SERVE 2

2 croissants
soya margarine to spread
¼ cucumber, peeled, seeded and finely sliced
225 g (8 oz) strawberries, hulled and sliced
50 g (2 oz) Mozzarella cheese, thinly sliced

Halve each croissant horizontally. Spread the bottom half with the margarine, then with a layer of cucumber, strawberry and Mozzarella slices. Grill under high heat until the cheese begins to melt. Replace the croissant top and serve immediately with the remaining strawberries.

Right: Sweetheart (*top*), page 92, Emerald Bites (*centre*), page 87 and Summer Strawberry (*bottom*), page 90

Sweetheart

⬦ V
346 kcal/1448 kJ
Fat: Low
Fibre: High

Serve as closed sandwiches for neat eating and carrying to picnic teas, but open to show the fruit for home consumption with a fork. The fruit salad filling is high in vitamins. From Helena Thomas, Wroughton.

TO SERVE 4

1 wholemeal fruit malt loaf, sliced
soya margarine to spread
1 banana, sliced
juice of ½ lemon
100 g (4 oz) strawberries, hulled and sliced
2 fresh figs, sliced
10 ml (2 tsp) clover honey (optional)

Cut the bread slices into heart shapes and spread with the margarine. Sprinkle the banana with lemon juice. Cover half the slices of bread with the strawberry, banana and fig slices. Drizzle the honey over the top, if liked. Cover with the remaining bread slices, pressing down well.

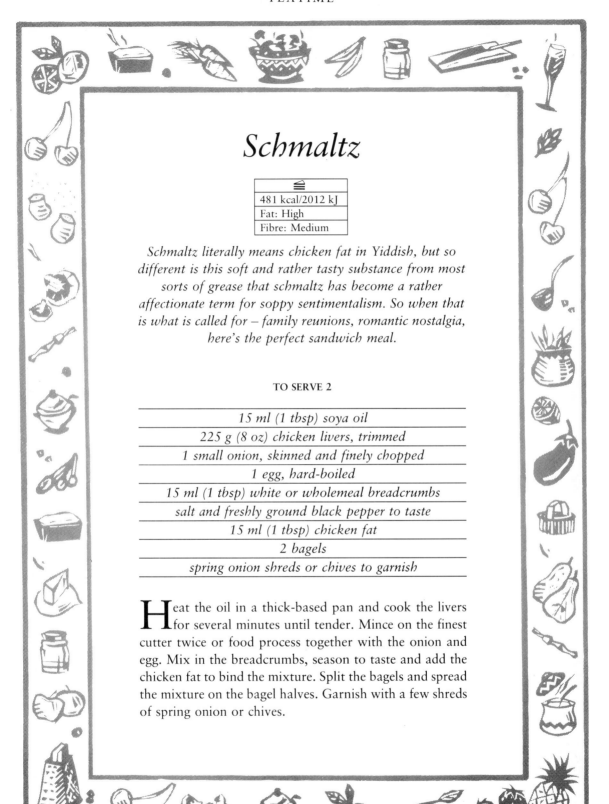

Schmaltz

⬘
481 kcal/2012 kJ
Fat: High
Fibre: Medium

Schmaltz literally means chicken fat in Yiddish, but so different is this soft and rather tasty substance from most sorts of grease that schmaltz has become a rather affectionate term for soppy sentimentalism. So when that is what is called for – family reunions, romantic nostalgia, here's the perfect sandwich meal.

TO SERVE 2

15 ml (1 tbsp) soya oil
225 g (8 oz) chicken livers, trimmed
1 small onion, skinned and finely chopped
1 egg, hard-boiled
15 ml (1 tbsp) white or wholemeal breadcrumbs
salt and freshly ground black pepper to taste
15 ml (1 tbsp) chicken fat
2 bagels
spring onion shreds or chives to garnish

Heat the oil in a thick-based pan and cook the livers for several minutes until tender. Mince on the finest cutter twice or food process together with the onion and egg. Mix in the breadcrumbs, season to taste and add the chicken fat to bind the mixture. Split the bagels and spread the mixture on the bagel halves. Garnish with a few shreds of spring onion or chives.

Paradisian

⌒	V
405 kcal/1694 kJ	
Fat: High	
Fibre: Medium	

Sandwich expert David Kenney, (aged 12), of Dyson Perrins C of E High School, recommends this sandwich for 'its inquisitive texture' – crunchy and smooth all at once. Lancashire cheese is ideal: grate rather than slice for tidy children's or travelling teas. An ideal sportsman's sandwich: restoring but not cloying. This is high in calories thanks to sheer size plus margarine, cheese and peanut butter. Good for high energy users only.

TO SERVE 1

soya margarine to spread
4 slices bread
25 g (1 oz) cheese, sliced or grated
1 tomato, sliced
peanut butter to spread
4 lettuce leaves
25 g (1 oz) cottage cheese

Spread the margarine on both sides of three of the slices of bread, and on one side only of the fourth. Cover the bread spread on one side only with the cheese and tomato. Add another slice of bread and spread with the peanut butter. On the next slice of bread, add the lettuce, then bread and finally spread the cottage cheese on top.

Picnic Sandwiches

Picnics never lose their charm, and should have charming sandwiches. This means sandwiches which are not only tasty, but carry with them some style, some atmosphere, some mood which will add to the enjoyment of the outing.

All that is in addition to two practical considerations. Picnic sandwiches must be portable: nothing too fragile. And they must be substantial – eating out-of-doors seems to make people hungrier.

As you might expect, sandwiches are the perfect picnic food. It's not just being able to eat them with your fingers: it's the simplicity of the idea, which suits the mood of the open air. Our selection aims to fit the bill, with the final thought that nothing should be too complicated to prepare.

Picnic ingredients

Your choice of picnic sandwich ingredients depends almost entirely on how much you are prepared to carry. The walker wants the maximum of solid nourishment out of the lightest lunchpack; but many other picnics take place only yards from car boots.

Picnic food easily gets warm in rucksacks, cars and trains. So any ingredient which might favour the growth of salmonella must be restricted to picnics where food will not spend more than 1–2 hours at such temperatures. So the lightweight, long-distance picnicker must choose carefully; cold bags are heavy to carry. The search for fillings that have more substance in least space, and are unlikely to set off food poisoning, eliminates both the bulky salad, and most cooked meat, especially chicken and pâté.

There are concentrated calorie fillings that are less likely to deteriorate. Hard cheese, avocados, sardines and other salted canned fish, peanut butter, nuts and seeds, chocolate, olive paste (tapenade) and salted meat, from bacon to

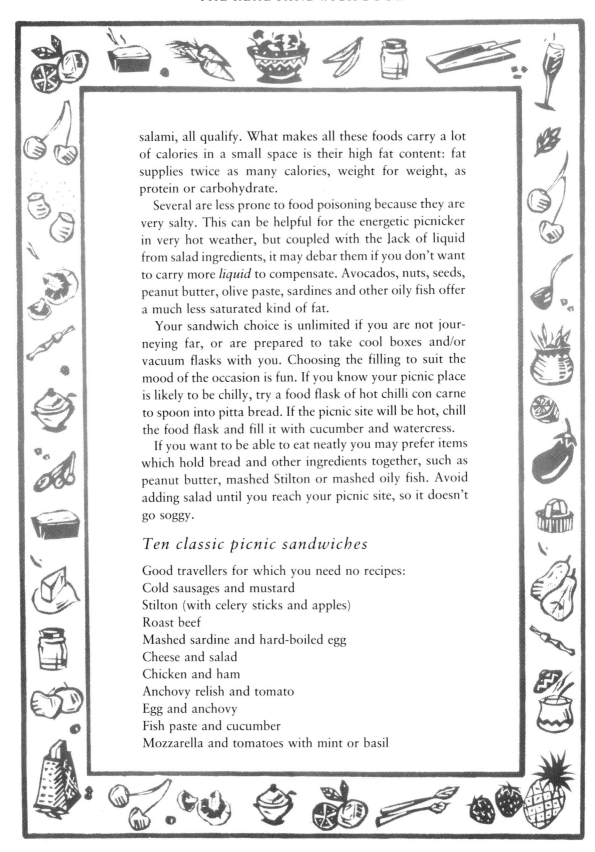

salami, all qualify. What makes all these foods carry a lot of calories in a small space is their high fat content: fat supplies twice as many calories, weight for weight, as protein or carbohydrate.

Several are less prone to food poisoning because they are very salty. This can be helpful for the energetic picnicker in very hot weather, but coupled with the lack of liquid from salad ingredients, it may debar them if you don't want to carry more *liquid* to compensate. Avocados, nuts, seeds, peanut butter, olive paste, sardines and other oily fish offer a much less saturated kind of fat.

Your sandwich choice is unlimited if you are not journeying far, or are prepared to take cool boxes and/or vacuum flasks with you. Choosing the filling to suit the mood of the occasion is fun. If you know your picnic place is likely to be chilly, try a food flask of hot chilli con carne to spoon into pitta bread. If the picnic site will be hot, chill the food flask and fill it with cucumber and watercress.

If you want to be able to eat neatly you may prefer items which hold bread and other ingredients together, such as peanut butter, mashed Stilton or mashed oily fish. Avoid adding salad until you reach your picnic site, so it doesn't go soggy.

Ten classic picnic sandwiches

Good travellers for which you need no recipes:
Cold sausages and mustard
Stilton (with celery sticks and apples)
Roast beef
Mashed sardine and hard-boiled egg
Cheese and salad
Chicken and ham
Anchovy relish and tomato
Egg and anchovy
Fish paste and cucumber
Mozzarella and tomatoes with mint or basil

Club Med

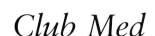

⟐	⟐	V
404 kcal/1689 kJ		
Fat: Low		
Fibre: High		

What a stunner! Sundried tomatoes are worth hunting for, as they do have a special flavour of the sun – but 'beef' tomatoes are what to use if your hunt is in vain. Tapenade is easy-to-make olive paste (see recipe, page 45). It is garlicky, so debarring this dish from cream teas and boardroom lunches, but ideal for parties and picnics. This is a balanced dish, provided you take up the option of mustard and cress, and use it generously. From Diana Cooper, Southampton.

TO SERVE 1

2 slices Italian-style white bread
1 slice wholemeal bread
soya margarine, to spread
tapenade (see page 45)
mustard and cress or alfalfa sprouts (optional)
10 ml (2 tsp) sundried tomato purée
50 g (2 oz) goat's cheese
chopped fresh oregano or parsley (optional)
a handful of black olives to serve

Spread the bread with the margarine, the wholemeal bread on both sides. Cover a slice of white bread with tapenade and mustard and cress or alfalfa sprouts, if using. Top with the wholemeal bread, spread this with the tomato purée, followed by the goat's cheese and herbs, if using. Cover with the remaining white slice. Eat with olives.

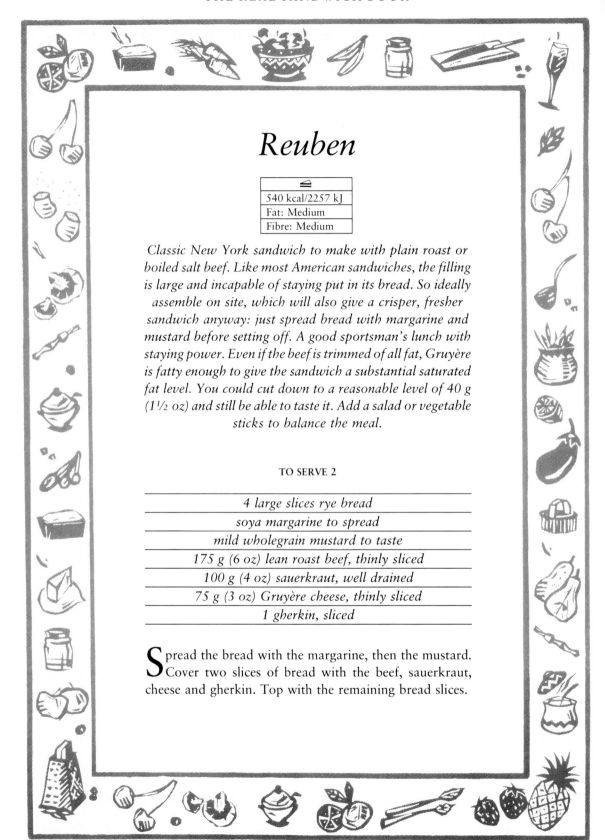

Reuben

🥪
540 kcal/2257 kJ
Fat: Medium
Fibre: Medium

Classic New York sandwich to make with plain roast or boiled salt beef. Like most American sandwiches, the filling is large and incapable of staying put in its bread. So ideally assemble on site, which will also give a crisper, fresher sandwich anyway: just spread bread with margarine and mustard before setting off. A good sportsman's lunch with staying power. Even if the beef is trimmed of all fat, Gruyère is fatty enough to give the sandwich a substantial saturated fat level. You could cut down to a reasonable level of 40 g (1½ oz) and still be able to taste it. Add a salad or vegetable sticks to balance the meal.

TO SERVE 2

4 large slices rye bread
soya margarine to spread
mild wholegrain mustard to taste
175 g (6 oz) lean roast beef, thinly sliced
100 g (4 oz) sauerkraut, well drained
75 g (3 oz) Gruyère cheese, thinly sliced
1 gherkin, sliced

Spread the bread with the margarine, then the mustard. Cover two slices of bread with the beef, sauerkraut, cheese and gherkin. Top with the remaining bread slices.

Legionnaire

🍞	ᴠ
450 kcal/1879 kJ	
Fat: Low	
Fibre: High	

The Roman approach to beans – and the kind of sandwich that kept the troops going when they came to Britain. Team with other Mediterranean dishes with sharper flavours – or just a jar of olives and chunks of beef tomato. The key to success is plenty of fresh herbs and lemon juice.

TO SERVE 2

100 g (4 oz) white haricot beans, soaked overnight
15 ml(1 tbsp) soya oil
30 ml (2 tbsp) mixed fresh herbs, eg tarragon, parsley, thyme and marjoram
juice of ½ lemon
freshly ground black pepper
dash of anchovy sauce (optional)
2 wholemeal pitta bread
soya margarine to spread
4 large lettuce leaves

Drain the beans, checking carefully for small stones or blackened beans. Place the beans in a saucepan and cover with fresh water. Bring to the boil, cover and simmer for 45–60 minutes until tender. Purée or mash the beans with oil, herbs and only just enough cooking liquid to give a stiff mixture in a blender or food processor. Add the lemon juice, pepper and anchovy sauce, if using, all to taste. Split the pitta bread and spread with the margarine. Line pitta pockets with lettuce and spoon in the bean mixture.

Forfar the Greek

≙
322 kcal/1347 kJ
Fat: High
Fibre: Medium

*Greek salad in a pitta, as delicious on a Hebridean ferry
as on an Aegean beach. For easy eating, shred ingredients
a little finer than you might for the salad bowl at home,
and ideally keep filling and bread apart until just before
the picnic starts. Feta cheese is in the same high league for
saturated fat as other hard cheeses, but its extreme saltiness
means you can use small amounts and still get its flavour.
Tuna oil is always low in saturates, although of course as
high in calories as other fats. From Jackie Sutherland,
Forfar.*

TO SERVE 4

200 g (7 oz) can tuna in oil
½ green pepper, seeded and chopped
4 spring onions, trimmed and chopped
10-cm (4-inch) piece cucumber, diced
1 egg, hard-boiled, roughly chopped
2–3 tomatoes, skinned and chopped
50 g (2 oz) feta cheese, diced
6 black olives, stoned and chopped
freshly ground black pepper
4 round mini pitta bread

Drain about half the oil from the tuna. Mash the tuna
with all the other ingredients, adding pepper to taste.
Warm the pitta bread. Slit and fill the pitta pockets with
the mixture.

Bagels and Lox

| 251 kcal/1049 kJ |
| Fat: Low |
| Fibre: High |

What makes a bagel different from an ordinary roll? The way that it is cooked. The 'roll with a hole' of dough is allowed to rise, then poached in water for a few minutes, puffing up far more, before being baked. The result is a unique texture and glazed finish. Bagels with lox – from the Yiddish laks for smoked salmon – started as a Jewish speciality. This dish is low in saturated fat (provided low fat cheese is used), high in calcium and essential fatty acids. Try to choose cheese and salmon that are not too salty, and team this dish with chunks of pepper and green cucumber to provide some vitamin C.

TO SERVE 4

4 bagels
225 g (8 oz) low or medium fat soft cheese
150 g (5 oz) smoked salmon
freshly ground black pepper
15 ml (1 tbsp) chopped fresh dill (optional)
4 lemon wedges to serve

Split the bagels. Spread each half thickly with the cheese, then the salmon, finishing with pepper and dill, if using. Serve as open sandwiches, if liked, with lemon wedges.

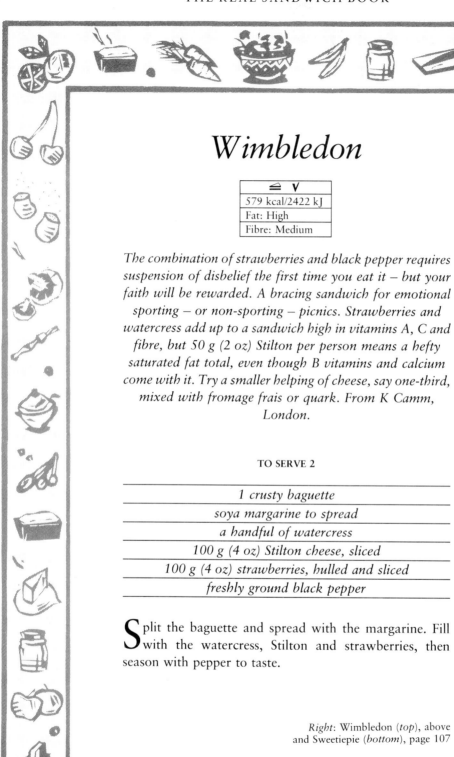

Wimbledon

⌂ V
579 kcal/2422 kJ
Fat: High
Fibre: Medium

The combination of strawberries and black pepper requires suspension of disbelief the first time you eat it – but your faith will be rewarded. A bracing sandwich for emotional sporting – or non-sporting – picnics. Strawberries and watercress add up to a sandwich high in vitamins A, C and fibre, but 50 g (2 oz) Stilton per person means a hefty saturated fat total, even though B vitamins and calcium come with it. Try a smaller helping of cheese, say one-third, mixed with fromage frais or quark. From K Camm, London.

TO SERVE 2

1 crusty baguette
soya margarine to spread
a handful of watercress
100 g (4 oz) Stilton cheese, sliced
100 g (4 oz) strawberries, hulled and sliced
freshly ground black pepper

Split the baguette and spread with the margarine. Fill with the watercress, Stilton and strawberries, then season with pepper to taste.

Right: Wimbledon (*top*), above and Sweetiepie (*bottom*), page 107

Pan Bagna

545 kcal/2278 kJ
Fat: Medium
Fibre: High

Tastes of the Mediterranean based on tomatoes and garlic, this dish travels well because the filling is meant to soak through the bread. Ideal for vegetarians, who can simply omit anchovies and replace with fat Spanish capers. Salt is the only potential problem of this high vitamin, low saturates sandwich. It is fairly high in calories too, although mainly from unsaturated fats. To reduce these, halve the amount of oil.

TO SERVE 4

1 long French bread or 2 granary batons
1–2 garlic cloves, skinned and crushed
30 ml (2 tbsp) soya oil
30 ml (2 tbsp) oil from anchovy tin
2.5 ml (½ tsp) mild French mustard
pinch of sugar
salt and freshly ground black pepper to taste
juice of ½ lemon
15 ml (1 tbsp) wine vinegar
450 g (1 lb) beefsteak tomatoes, sliced
1 Spanish onion, skinned and finely sliced
1 green pepper, seeded and thinly sliced
1 red pepper, seeded and thinly sliced
25 g (1 oz) anchovy fillets, drained and halved lengthways
15 black olives, stoned
2 eggs, hard-boiled and thinly sliced

→

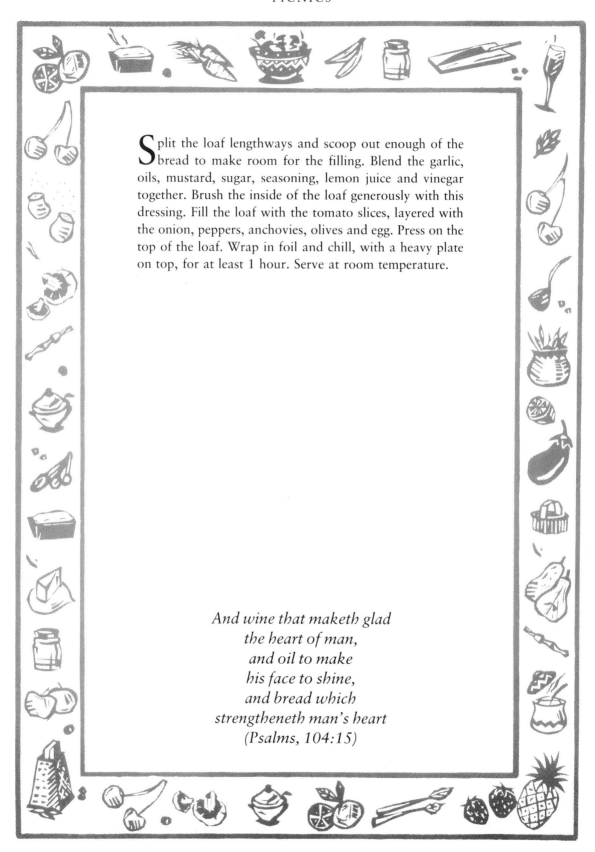

Split the loaf lengthways and scoop out enough of the bread to make room for the filling. Blend the garlic, oils, mustard, sugar, seasoning, lemon juice and vinegar together. Brush the inside of the loaf generously with this dressing. Fill the loaf with the tomato slices, layered with the onion, peppers, anchovies, olives and egg. Press on the top of the loaf. Wrap in foil and chill, with a heavy plate on top, for at least 1 hour. Serve at room temperature.

And wine that maketh glad
the heart of man,
and oil to make
his face to shine,
and bread which
strengtheneth man's heart
(Psalms, 104:15)

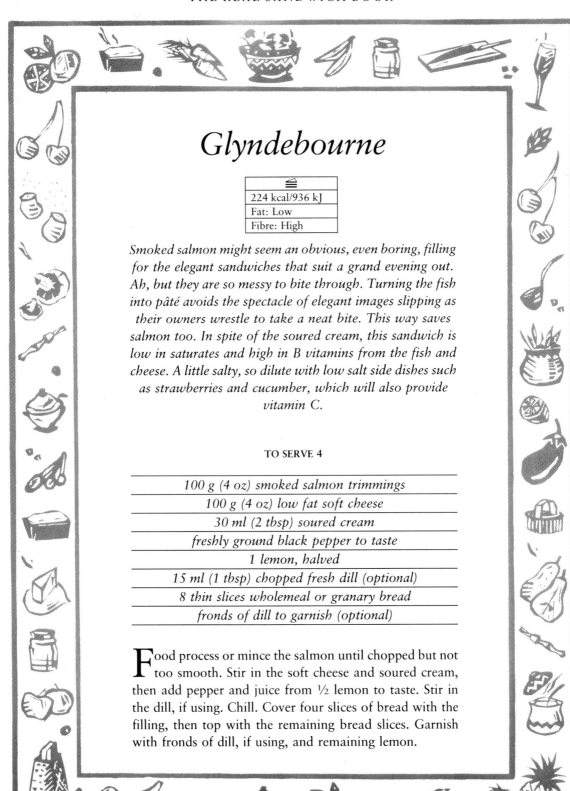

Glyndebourne

≙
224 kcal/936 kJ
Fat: Low
Fibre: High

*Smoked salmon might seem an obvious, even boring, filling
for the elegant sandwiches that suit a grand evening out.
Ah, but they are so messy to bite through. Turning the fish
into pâté avoids the spectacle of elegant images slipping as
their owners wrestle to take a neat bite. This way saves
salmon too. In spite of the soured cream, this sandwich is
low in saturates and high in B vitamins from the fish and
cheese. A little salty, so dilute with low salt side dishes such
as strawberries and cucumber, which will also provide
vitamin C.*

TO SERVE 4

100 g (4 oz) smoked salmon trimmings
100 g (4 oz) low fat soft cheese
30 ml (2 tbsp) soured cream
freshly ground black pepper to taste
1 lemon, halved
15 ml (1 tbsp) chopped fresh dill (optional)
8 thin slices wholemeal or granary bread
fronds of dill to garnish (optional)

Food process or mince the salmon until chopped but not
too smooth. Stir in the soft cheese and soured cream,
then add pepper and juice from ½ lemon to taste. Stir in
the dill, if using. Chill. Cover four slices of bread with the
filling, then top with the remaining bread slices. Garnish
with fronds of dill, if using, and remaining lemon.

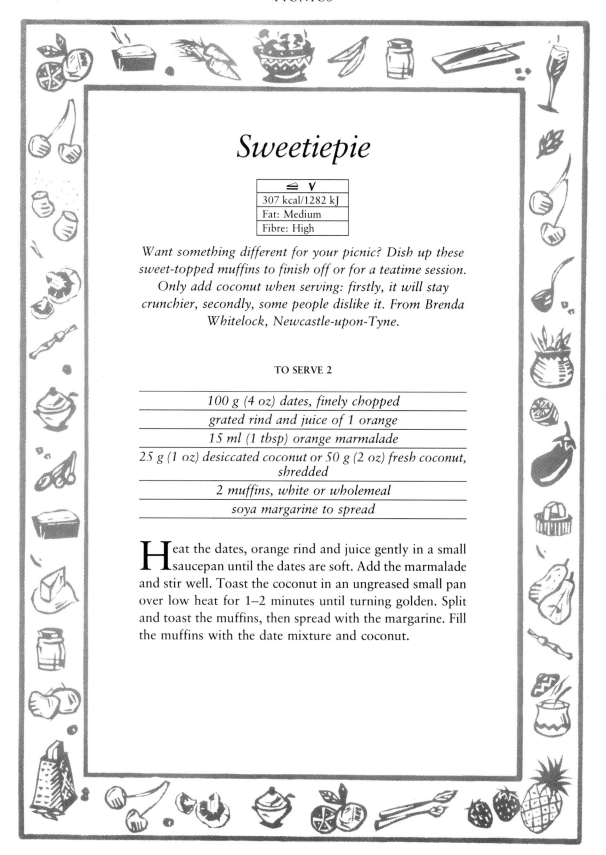

Sweetiepie

⊴ V
307 kcal/1282 kJ
Fat: Medium
Fibre: High

*Want something different for your picnic? Dish up these
sweet-topped muffins to finish off or for a teatime session.
Only add coconut when serving: firstly, it will stay
crunchier, secondly, some people dislike it. From Brenda
Whitelock, Newcastle-upon-Tyne.*

TO SERVE 2

100 g (4 oz) dates, finely chopped

grated rind and juice of 1 orange

15 ml (1 tbsp) orange marmalade

*25 g (1 oz) desiccated coconut or 50 g (2 oz) fresh coconut,
shredded*

2 muffins, white or wholemeal

soya margarine to spread

Heat the dates, orange rind and juice gently in a small
saucepan until the dates are soft. Add the marmalade
and stir well. Toast the coconut in an ungreased small pan
over low heat for 1–2 minutes until turning golden. Split
and toast the muffins, then spread with the margarine. Fill
the muffins with the date mixture and coconut.

Children's Parties

Every recipe in this section has been suggested by a child and some are accompanied by their illustrations. So what do younger children like best at parties? Food with built-in fantasy, it seems. Buses, butterflies or beings from outer space give familiar ingredients a party-ish excitement utterly lacking from plain sandwiches.

Big sandwiches make a lovely splash at parties for young children, but don't expect guests to tackle a large item. They may be positively alarmed by a massive plateful. So alongside your impressive butterfly sandwiches, provide some mini-butties. Follow up by chopping the showpieces into manageable helpings, just as if they were a cake.

A sandwich idea can give you a theme for the rest of the food too, for instance our Egyptian mummy sandwiches (gruesome as they may seem).

Older children may want food with a more sophisticated image. But like all of us, they like someone making a special effort for them. So stir-fry Dan Macs, ratatouille and ham sandwiches or special chicken cater for children who want something different. Many sandwiches from the Entertaining chapter suit teenage parties. All sandwiches are better for being colourful. For children, that's twice as important.

Children's parties ingredients

The key to sandwich success is providing a variety of flavours in such a way that children can avoid ingredients they don't like. The party spirit may sweep some children into trying new foods, and widening their repertoire. Others react by becoming extra-choosy. A party is not the time to argue over food.

Our recipes rarely use more unusual ingredients than you'd find in any sandwich bar. And many delicious ordinary sandwiches made from them need no recipes.

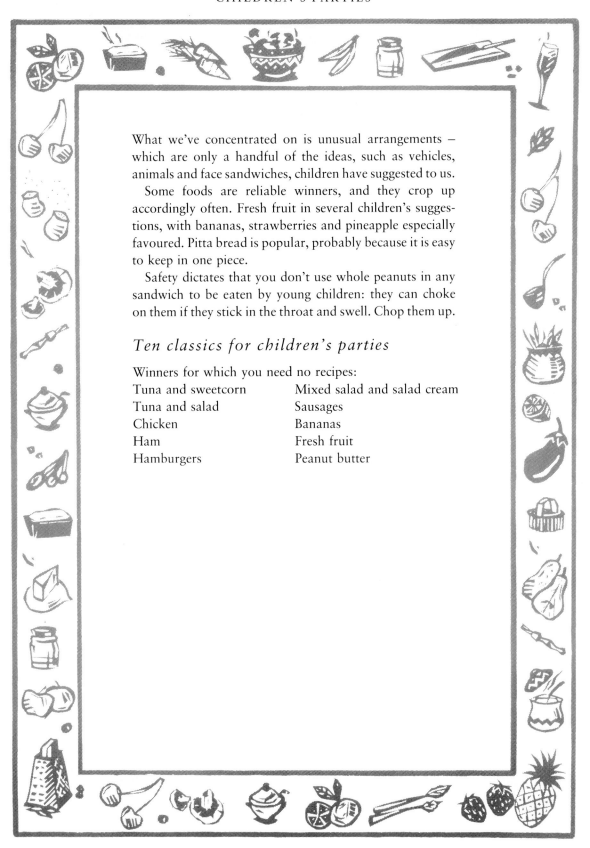

What we've concentrated on is unusual arrangements – which are only a handful of the ideas, such as vehicles, animals and face sandwiches, children have suggested to us.

Some foods are reliable winners, and they crop up accordingly often. Fresh fruit in several children's suggestions, with bananas, strawberries and pineapple especially favoured. Pitta bread is popular, probably because it is easy to keep in one piece.

Safety dictates that you don't use whole peanuts in any sandwich to be eaten by young children: they can choke on them if they stick in the throat and swell. Chop them up.

Ten classics for children's parties

Winners for which you need no recipes:

Tuna and sweetcorn	Mixed salad and salad cream
Tuna and salad	Sausages
Chicken	Bananas
Ham	Fresh fruit
Hamburgers	Peanut butter

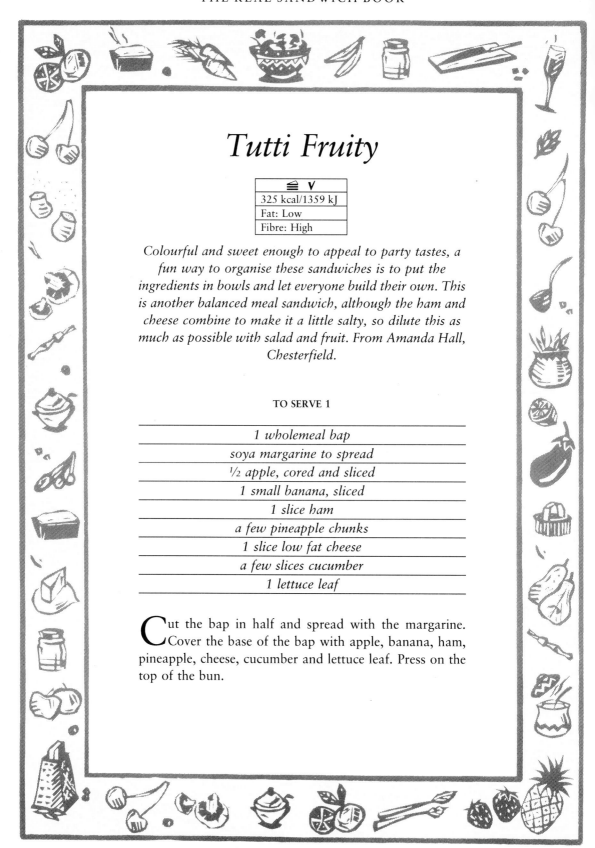

Tutti Fruity

≙ V
325 kcal/1359 kJ
Fat: Low
Fibre: High

Colourful and sweet enough to appeal to party tastes, a fun way to organise these sandwiches is to put the ingredients in bowls and let everyone build their own. This is another balanced meal sandwich, although the ham and cheese combine to make it a little salty, so dilute this as much as possible with salad and fruit. From Amanda Hall, Chesterfield.

TO SERVE 1

1 wholemeal bap
soya margarine to spread
½ apple, cored and sliced
1 small banana, sliced
1 slice ham
a few pineapple chunks
1 slice low fat cheese
a few slices cucumber
1 lettuce leaf

Cut the bap in half and spread with the margarine. Cover the base of the bap with apple, banana, ham, pineapple, cheese, cucumber and lettuce leaf. Press on the top of the bun.

Dan Mac

≜ ∨
433 kcal/1808 kJ
Fat: Medium
Fibre: High

Give children this colourful, quickly made 'burger'. Offer a slice of cheese on top as an extra – not to mention all the usual ketchups and relishes. This is not as substantial as higher-calorie burgers, so expect appetites to revive rapidly. But good news for vitamins provided these burgers are not overcooked. From Daniel Stark, Friesland School.

TO SERVE 4

50 g (2 oz) bamboo shoots
50 g (2 oz) beansprouts
3–4 mushrooms
50 g (2 oz) mange-tout or French beans
50 g (2 oz) broccoli or cauliflower
50 g (2 oz) carrots, peeled
60 ml (4 tbsp) soya oil
15 ml (1 tbsp) soy sauce
10 ml (2 tsp) sesame seed oil
4 pitta bread

→

Cut the bamboo shoots into slices the size of a large postage stamp. Wash the beansprouts in a bowl of cold water, discarding the husks etc that float to the surface. Leave the mushrooms whole if small, or cut in half if large. Chop the rest of the fresh vegetables into roughly the same size. Heat the soya oil in a wok or frying pan and stir-fry the vegetables for about 1½ minutes. Pour in the soy sauce and mix well together, then add the sesame seed oil. Toast the pitta bread, split open and fill the pitta pockets with the stir-fry mixture.

Bread is the staff of life
(17th century proverb)

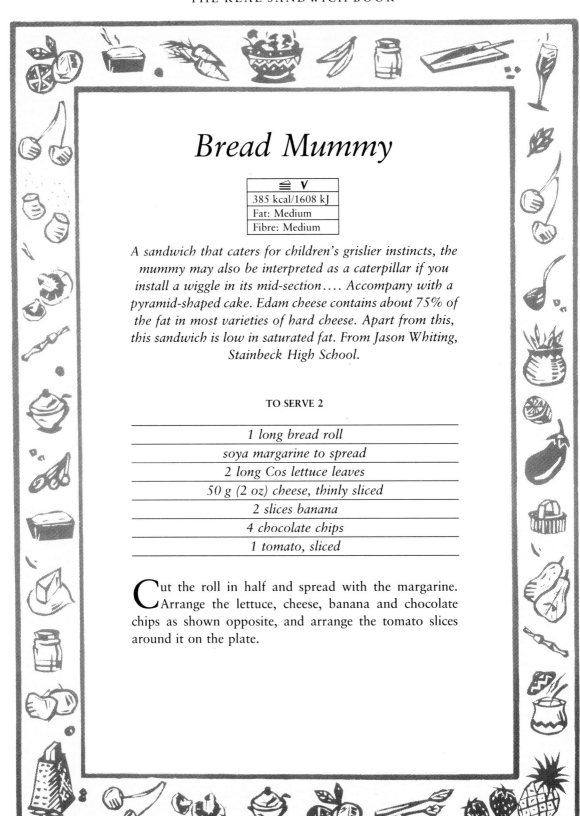

Bread Mummy

🍞 V
385 kcal/1608 kJ
Fat: Medium
Fibre: Medium

A sandwich that caters for children's grislier instincts, the mummy may also be interpreted as a caterpillar if you install a wiggle in its mid-section.... Accompany with a pyramid-shaped cake. Edam cheese contains about 75% of the fat in most varieties of hard cheese. Apart from this, this sandwich is low in saturated fat. From Jason Whiting, Stainbeck High School.

TO SERVE 2

1 long bread roll
soya margarine to spread
2 long Cos lettuce leaves
50 g (2 oz) cheese, thinly sliced
2 slices banana
4 chocolate chips
1 tomato, sliced

Cut the roll in half and spread with the margarine. Arrange the lettuce, cheese, banana and chocolate chips as shown opposite, and arrange the tomato slices around it on the plate.

What's the difference
between a hero and a submarine?
Just the name it seems.
Both are favourite
American names for big sandwiches
usually combining substantial amounts of
meat, cheese and salad in long rolls.
If you think the roll
has a submarine shape,
you call it a submarine.
If you think it takes a hero
to eat so much,
you call it that.

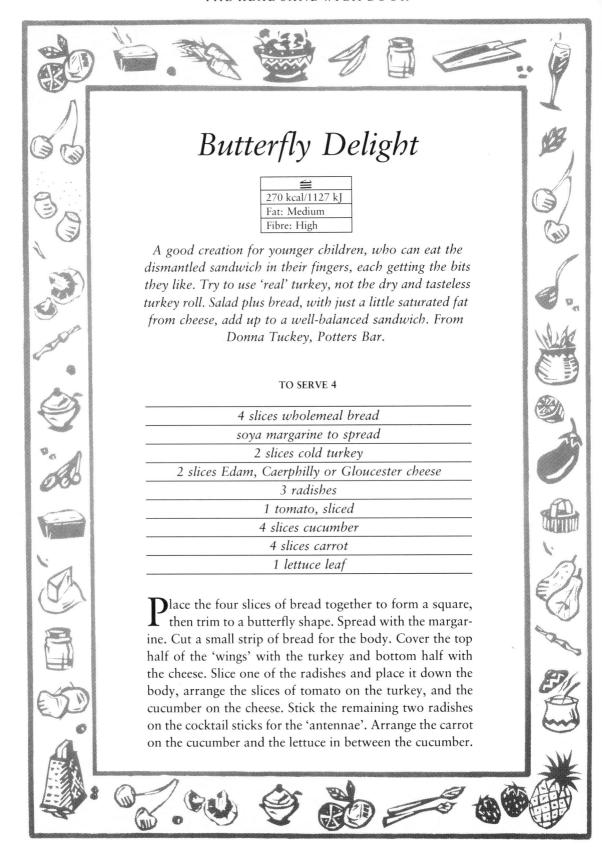

Butterfly Delight

≡
270 kcal/1127 kJ
Fat: Medium
Fibre: High

A good creation for younger children, who can eat the dismantled sandwich in their fingers, each getting the bits they like. Try to use 'real' turkey, not the dry and tasteless turkey roll. Salad plus bread, with just a little saturated fat from cheese, add up to a well-balanced sandwich. From Donna Tuckey, Potters Bar.

TO SERVE 4

4 slices wholemeal bread
soya margarine to spread
2 slices cold turkey
2 slices Edam, Caerphilly or Gloucester cheese
3 radishes
1 tomato, sliced
4 slices cucumber
4 slices carrot
1 lettuce leaf

Place the four slices of bread together to form a square, then trim to a butterfly shape. Spread with the margarine. Cut a small strip of bread for the body. Cover the top half of the 'wings' with the turkey and bottom half with the cheese. Slice one of the radishes and place it down the body, arrange the slices of tomato on the turkey, and the cucumber on the cheese. Stick the remaining two radishes on the cocktail sticks for the 'antennae'. Arrange the carrot on the cucumber and the lettuce in between the cucumber.

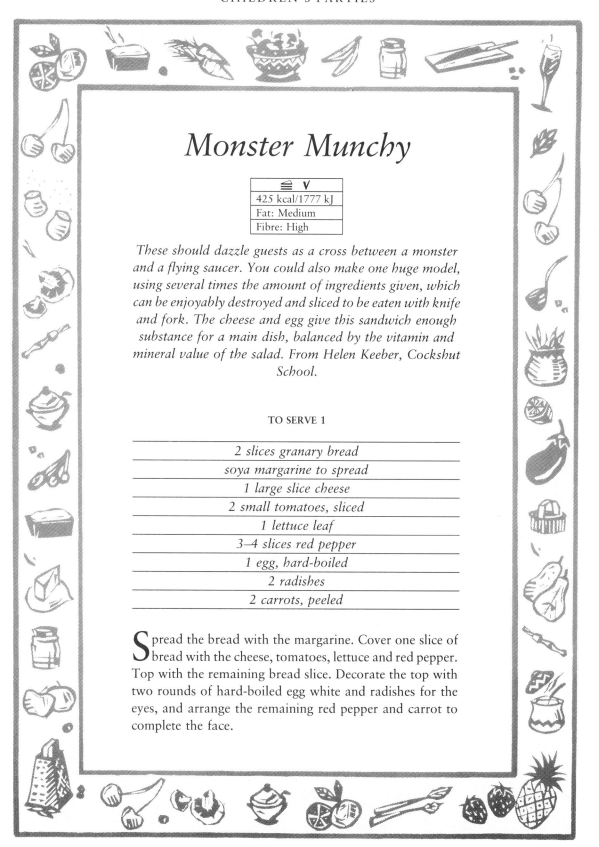

Monster Munchy

◸ V
425 kcal/1777 kJ
Fat: Medium
Fibre: High

These should dazzle guests as a cross between a monster and a flying saucer. You could also make one huge model, using several times the amount of ingredients given, which can be enjoyably destroyed and sliced to be eaten with knife and fork. The cheese and egg give this sandwich enough substance for a main dish, balanced by the vitamin and mineral value of the salad. From Helen Keeber, Cockshut School.

TO SERVE 1

2 slices granary bread
soya margarine to spread
1 large slice cheese
2 small tomatoes, sliced
1 lettuce leaf
3–4 slices red pepper
1 egg, hard-boiled
2 radishes
2 carrots, peeled

Spread the bread with the margarine. Cover one slice of bread with the cheese, tomatoes, lettuce and red pepper. Top with the remaining bread slice. Decorate the top with two rounds of hard-boiled egg white and radishes for the eyes, and arrange the remaining red pepper and carrot to complete the face.

Tuna Bus

≜
254 kcal/1062 kJ
Fat: Medium
Fibre: Medium

A model for many other style of vehicle to make with rolls and imagination. Cut the tomato slices thickly, and with the help of cocktail sticks as axles, the bus can really roll. From Trisha Ann Peck, Potters Bar.

TO SERVE 1

1 hoagie roll
soya margarine to spread
2 long lettuce leaves
25 g (1 oz) mature Cheddar cheese, grated
1 eating apple, diced
75 g (3 oz) tuna or liver sausage
4 tomato slices, thickly cut

Cut the roll in half and spread with the margarine. Layer the lettuce leaves, cheese, apple and tuna or sausage as shown below, then add the tomato 'wheels'.

Right: Sleepy Bears (*top*), page 124
and Butterfly Delight (*bottom*), page 116

Minted Ratatouille

⊜ V
433 kcal/1808 kJ
Fat: High
Fibre: High

Ham meets ratatouille to make a 'face' sandwich complete with pink tongue, green eyes and gruesome appeal to children who can enjoy a spot of harmless cannibalism. Pork is considered fatty, but fat-trimmed ham is one of the lowest fat meats. Because the meat is salty, avoid salting the ratatouille, giving this sandwich a good fibre and vitamin content. From Samantha Smith, Potters Bar.

TO SERVE 1

½ onion, skinned
½ green pepper, seeded
½ red pepper, seeded
1 small courgette
50 g (2 oz) mushrooms
2 tomatoes, skinned, seeded and quartered
10 ml (2 tsp) soya oil
salt and freshly ground black pepper
15 ml (1 tbsp) chopped fresh mint
2 slices wholemeal bread
soya margarine to spread
2 slices ham

→

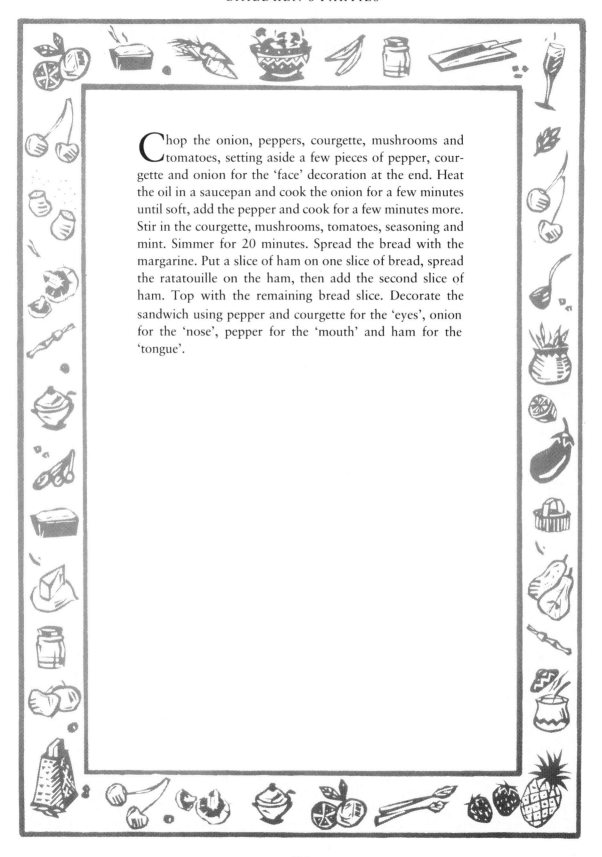

Chop the onion, peppers, courgette, mushrooms and tomatoes, setting aside a few pieces of pepper, courgette and onion for the 'face' decoration at the end. Heat the oil in a saucepan and cook the onion for a few minutes until soft, add the pepper and cook for a few minutes more. Stir in the courgette, mushrooms, tomatoes, seasoning and mint. Simmer for 20 minutes. Spread the bread with the margarine. Put a slice of ham on one slice of bread, spread the ratatouille on the ham, then add the second slice of ham. Top with the remaining bread slice. Decorate the sandwich using pepper and courgette for the 'eyes', onion for the 'nose', pepper for the 'mouth' and ham for the 'tongue'.

Horn of Plenty

380 kcal/1587 kJ
Fat: High
Fibre: High

A grown-up sandwich for would-be sophisticates: any adults present will finish these off. If the rolls won't stay rolled, tie them up with narrow strips of ham or other cooked meat. A 'lean' sandwich which can be eaten without any sense of guilt: provided you don't polish off handfuls of peanuts while making them. From Helen Mitchell, Potters Bar.

TO SERVE 2

4 slices wholemeal bread

yogurt dressing:

150 ml (¼ pint) natural yogurt

10 ml (2 tsp) soya oil

5 ml (1 tsp) apricot jam or ½ peach, grated

5 ml (1 tsp) honey

15 ml (1 tbsp) lemon juice

5 ml (1 tsp) curry powder

salt and freshly ground black pepper to taste

filling:

75 g (3 oz) cold cooked chicken

a few sultanas and peanuts

1 stick celery, sliced

decoration:

½ small carrot, peeled and sliced

a few strips of apple peel

2 gherkins, one sliced lengthways

1 radish, finely sliced

→

Mix all the ingredients for the yogurt dressing together. Coat the chicken, sultanas and peanuts and celery with this dressing. Spoon the mixture on to the slices of bread and roll as shown, then secure. Decorate the round ends with carrot, apple peel, gherkins and radish.

Sleepy Bears

⏥ ∨
173 kcal/723 kJ
Fat: Low
Fibre: High

This sandwich-making certainly takes longer, but it is more interesting when building shapes like this. A good sandwich for younger children's parties. Apart from the sugar on the cherries, a very healthy filling. From Eleanor Bennett, Friesland School.

TO SERVE 6

1 small banana

2 rings pineapple

1 small apple

a few glacé cherries with natural colouring

1 small can apricot halves in natural juice, drained

6 small wholemeal pitta bread

First prepare the fruit, by cutting them into the shapes for the head. Chop the remaining fruit and put on one side. Place the pitta bread under the grill. Do not toast them, just heat slightly on both sides. Cut a slit across each pitta bread, making sure you do not cut through to the other side. Put your fingers in the middle to make a pouch. Place some chunks of the fruit inside it and tuck one chunk into the top to make the 'pillow'. Put the apricot half on to the pillow so it is lying on the slit, then place the banana 'ears' in position. Cut two little dents in the apricot to rest the 'eyes' on, and do the same for the 'mouth'. Position the pineapple 'paws', then brush the fruit with the apricot juice.

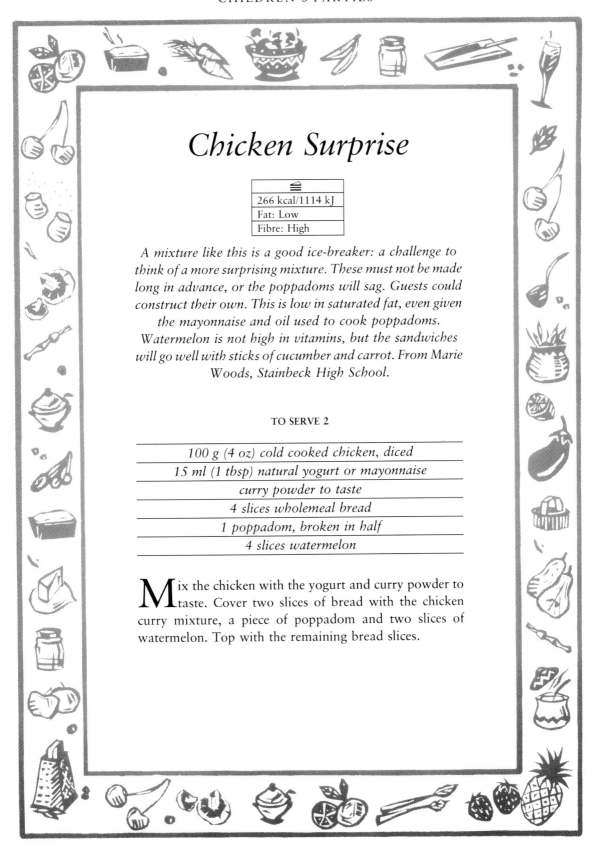

Chicken Surprise

≜
266 kcal/1114 kJ
Fat: Low
Fibre: High

A mixture like this is a good ice-breaker: a challenge to think of a more surprising mixture. These must not be made long in advance, or the poppadoms will sag. Guests could construct their own. This is low in saturated fat, even given the mayonnaise and oil used to cook poppadoms. Watermelon is not high in vitamins, but the sandwiches will go well with sticks of cucumber and carrot. From Marie Woods, Stainbeck High School.

TO SERVE 2

100 g (4 oz) cold cooked chicken, diced
15 ml (1 tbsp) natural yogurt or mayonnaise
curry powder to taste
4 slices wholemeal bread
1 poppadom, broken in half
4 slices watermelon

Mix the chicken with the yogurt and curry powder to taste. Cover two slices of bread with the chicken curry mixture, a piece of poppadom and two slices of watermelon. Top with the remaining bread slices.

Valentines

≙ √
72 kcal/300 kJ
Fat: Low
Fibre: High

A sandwich for the fussy teenage girl who wants something to look at as much as eat. If strawberries are not in season, cut hearts from kiwi fruit or peaches with a petits four cutter. This is really fruit salad on a sandwich and, provided you don't go wild with margarine, eminently suitable for teenage diets. From Retha Begum, Glamorgan.

TO SERVE 4

2 slices wholemeal bread
soya margarine to spread
1 small banana, sliced
lemon juice
8 large strawberries, hulled and sliced

Cut the bread slices in half diagonally to form triangles, then spread with the margarine. Arrange the slices of banana, sprinkled with lemon juice, and strawberry as shown below.

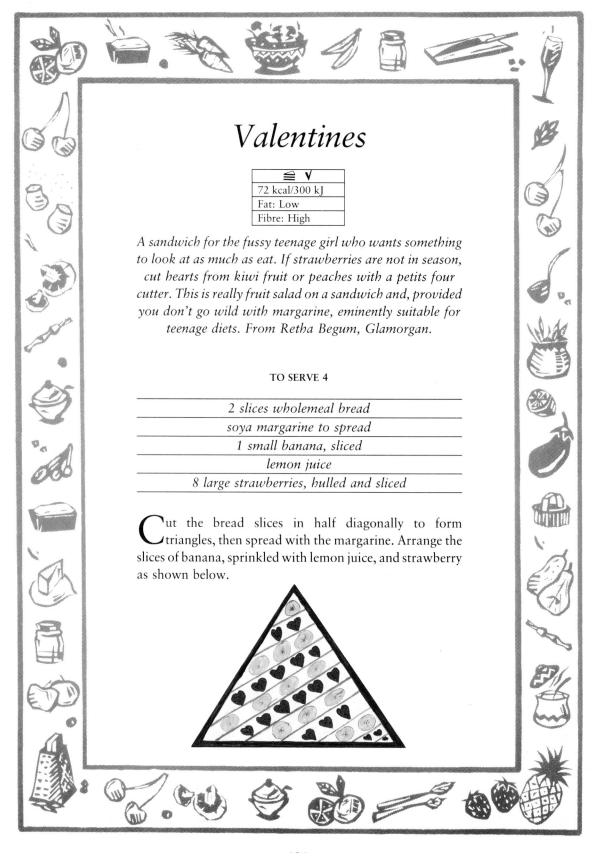

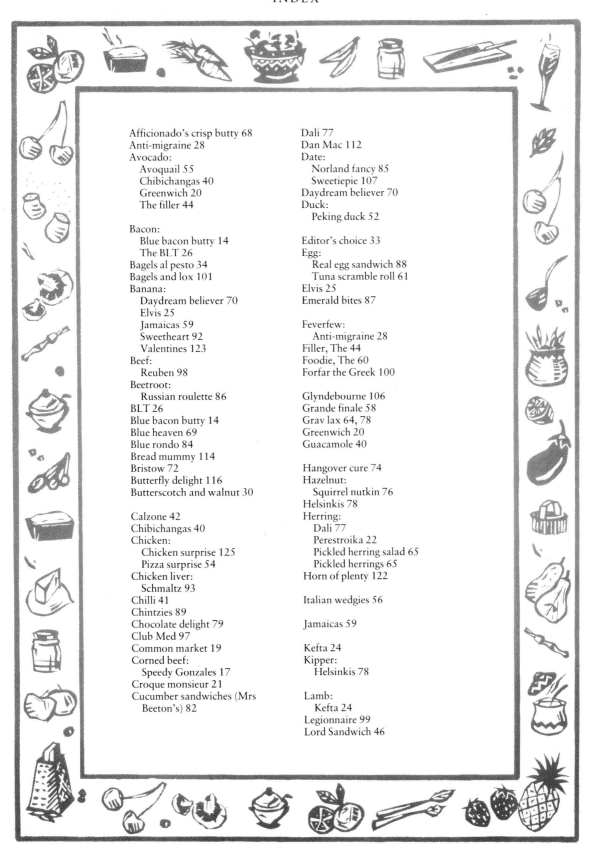

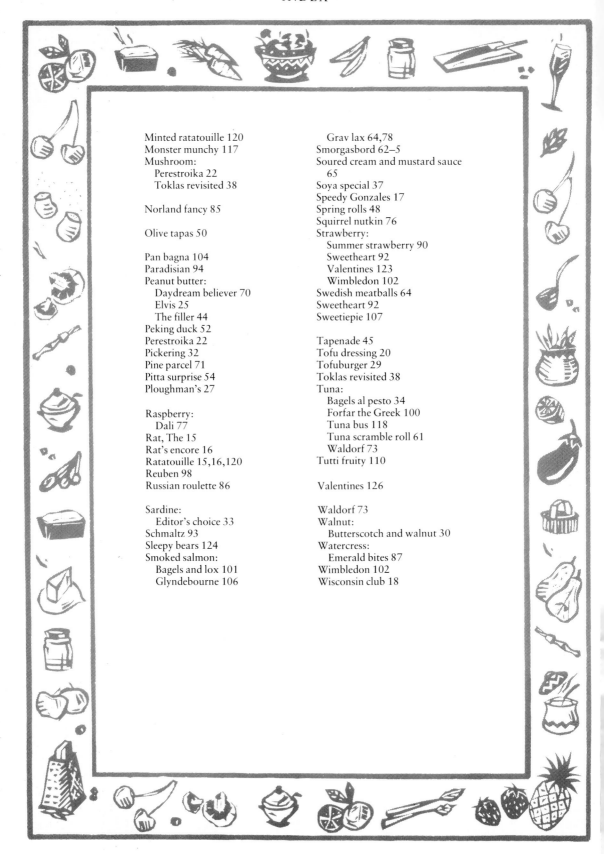